Praise for

Protecting Yourself from Emc

"Many have written lately about the manipulative sorts who know how to manage impressions but heartlessly prey on your sensibilities to get the better of you. But Steven describes these emotional predators with uncommon clarity and accuracy, in an excellent writing style, and offers spot-on practical advice on how to best protect yourself to boot. A must read!"

George Simon, Ph.D,
author of *In Sheep's Clothing* and
Character Disturbance: The Phenomenon of Our Age

"I've read so many books identifying issues with NO solutions or strategies on what to do. You presented very practical and realistic strategies that are within grasp and will make a difference. I got answers, not more questions. You presented real life things to do. Thank you for writing this book and getting this important information out into the world."

Kimberly M - artist, escapee from an abusive relationship

"This is excellent. The way you explain psychological terms such as 'empathy' is really helpful for a lay person like me. And it really helped that you call out the deficiencies of more traditional therapies in dealing with emotional predators. I wish therapists I saw had read your book. Your examples are great."

Bryan B - senior business attorney

"Like no other book I know, *Protecting Yourself from Emotional Predators* gives my patients a language to speak about their anguish from traumatic encounters with manipulative and abusive people, and a framework for how to respond. It empowers them to act.

Wolhandler's book is easy and quick to read. The writing pulls in the reader. His thesis is very clear and the rare times he uses jargon, he defines it clearly (projection, projective identification, lying by omission, etc.).

This fascinating new work is essential reading for anyone who needs help dealing with a manipulative or abusive person and an invaluable adjunct to my psychotherapy work with these patients."

Margaret Jacobs, LCSW, JD
Psychotherapist and Psychoanalyst, New York, NY

"Not since George Simon has this topic been broached with such clarity. Wolhandler takes this topic head on and reminds his readers that Emotional Predators are both real and abundant in to-day's society.

Protecting Yourself from Emotional Predators is a must read that reminds the reader that the only one who can protect themself from certain types of people is the reader, so take heed of the simple tools this book offers. Stop second guessing yourself and start asking powerful questions to ascertain whether or not you have been made a target of an Emotional Predator."

Sharon Tessier, MA MS, PhD (cand)
Retired Wellness Coaching Coordinator
Integrative Health Care Program
Metropolitan State University

"Written from a rare position of wisdom. Like no other self-help book I've encountered. Articulate, intelligent, and scientific while at the same time readable and relevant.... I mean relevant! I've learned an astounding amount. A real gem!!"

Laurence A - entrepreneur

"A welcome addition to the self-help literature.

Having worked with patients who've been mistreated, I know how difficult it is for them to see their situation and their tormentor clearly. These patients will benefit from your forceful style of writing and your uncompromising attitude toward the problem of victimization and its resolution.

Your book gets to the heart of the matter of helping the patient recognize how the predator operates and the importance of "protecting yourself right now." You provide a stark but true image of the emotional predator as a land mine in the sunlit fields of your life. This book is for people that just don't get that a person that they love has the unvarnished intent to take advantage, do them harm and make them suffer. Until and unless this insight is achieved the chance of escaping victimization is almost impossible."

Bill Kotsch, Ph.D.
Clinical and Consulting Psychologist, Santa Fe, NM
Former
Core Faculty at Chicago School of Professional Psychology
Assistant Professor, Clinical Psychology at Baylor University
Post-Doctorate Fellow, Research Associate
and Lecturer at Vanderbilt University
Diplomat in Jungian Analysis at C. G. Jung Institute of Chicago

"This is great. It all rings true! Thank you! Realizing that other people don't think the way I do has been super helpful with my relations within my family - much more than three therapists were. I was always giving them one more chance and hoping they'd change. Now it really helps to know not to expect them to become different people."

Keith B - handyman, retired landscaper

"I really loved this! It speaks to me on a lot of levels and really rings true both for spotting predators and for neutralizing them. Takes narcissists/sociopaths/etc and puts them in a context I can understand and handle. I like how you say not to think of them as humans but rather predators with a human semblance that use human emotion as a lure/trap. I think a big problem with dealing with these kinds of people is that we don't understand what they're really like."

Emilie A - film producer

"This work offers an important perspective to mental/behavioral health issues that is not currently being addressed in our culture. It provides guidance to help people recognize and protect themselves from emotional predators. Wolhandler approaches this topic in accessible language and provides practical, accessible tools. Application of these ideas is important for the general public and for those in positions of authority in our social institutions (e.g., schools, faith community, justice, mental health, child welfare)."

Beverly Kingston, Ph.D.
Director and Senior Research Associate
Center for the Study and Prevention of Violence
Institute of Behavioral Science
University of Colorado Boulder

PROTECTING YOURSELF

from

EMOTIONAL PREDATORS

PROTECTING YOURSELF

from

EMOTIONAL PREDATORS

Neutralize the Users, Abusers and Manipulators Hidden Among Us

STEVEN J WOLHANDLER, JD, MA, LPC

 AMARE PRESS

PROTECTING YOURSELF from EMOTIONAL PREDATORS: Neutralize the Users, Abusers and Manipulators Hidden Among Us
Published by Amare Press, Boulder, Colorado

Copyright © 2018 Steven Wolhandler. All rights reserved.

No part of this book may be reproduced in any form or by any means, electronic or mechanical, including information storage and retrieval systems without permission in writing from the publisher or author, except by a reviewer who may quote passages in a review.

All images, logos, quotes, and trademarks included in this book are subject to use according to trademark and copyright laws of the United States of America.

Library of Congress Control Number: 2018909061

Author: Steven Wolhandler

PROTECTING YOURSELF from EMOTIONAL PREDATORS: Neutralize the Users, Abusers and Manipulators Hidden Among Us

ISBN-13: 978-0-692-16052-7
PSYCHOLOGY / Interpersonal Relations

All people and examples described in this book are composites based on actual people and events, but with all identifying attributes changed to protect anonymity and privacy. They are for purposes of illustration only and fictional, not biographical. While the relevant facts are accurate, any resemblance to actual people or events is coincidental. Mention of public figures is for illustration and does not imply any diagnosis or conclusions about them. Any perceived slights of actual people, places or entities are unintentional.

None of the advice or suggestions in this book are legal or medical advice. Consult the attorney of your choice for legal advice and the health care practitioner of your choice for medical advice, including advice about mental health and psychology.

QUANTITY PURCHASES: Schools, companies, professional groups, clubs, and other organizations may qualify for special terms when ordering quantities of this title. For information, email steven@emotionalpredators.com.

All rights reserved by Steven Wolhandler
This book is printed in the United States of America.

 AMARE PRESS

Table of Contents

◆

Acknowledgments

This book would not have happened without support and help from many people.

Thank you to all the patients, clients, family and colleagues who taught me so much about the true nature of hidden abusive manipulators. Many friends - too many to name - read early drafts and gave me valuable feedback, tempering the isolation of writing with caring connection and support. I love and appreciate you all.

This book draws on the work of Theodore Millon, Robert Hare, George Simon, Martha Stout, Albert Bernstein and others to whom I owe an immense debt.

I cannot adequately express my gratitude to Sharon Tessier, who midwifed this book out of me and sheparded it along its path to completion. No matter how busy with public service and her family, Sharon was always there for me with just the right feedback and encouragement. Lloyd Jassin, attorney extraordinaire, was relentlessly patient, generous, learned and wise. Paul Weidig gave me sage feedback and suggestions about every aspect of the project and steadied me as needed.

Many people patiently guided me through the publishing process. Thank you to Victoria Wolf for the artwork, Andrea Constantine for the layout, and Polly Letofsky who gently helped with every part of the publishing process.

Finally, I owe a huge debt to my daughter, Isabel, for her wise suggestions, maturity and tolerant understanding in the face of my periodic grumpiness, and also to Stella, who always puts things in a positive perspective.

◆

Author's Notes

All people and examples described in this book are composites based on actual people and events, but with all identifying attributes changed to protect anonymity and privacy. They are for purposes of illustration only and fictional, not biographical. While the relevant facts are accurate, any resemblance to actual people or events is coincidental. Mention of public figures is for illustration and does not imply any diagnosis or conclusions about them. Any slights of actual people, places or entities are unintentional.

None of the advice or suggestions in this book are legal or medical advice. Consult the attorney of your choice for legal advice and the health care practitioner of your choice for medical advice, including advice about mental health and psychology. The advice and suggestions in this book may or may not fit your particular situation. Use your own judgment about which, if any, to use.

Emotional Predators come in all genders. Rather than the awkward "he/she" or "he or she" construction for the third person singular, I've alternated randomly using "they," "he" and "she."

As you read this book, you may be reminded of people you know and public figures. It's useful to pay attention if that happens and use the examples from your own life, or perhaps from the world at large, to illustrate the ideas you are reading about. But, as you'll see, if you recognize some of the traits and behaviors of Emotional Predators in *yourself*, and this arouses guilt and shame, it's a pretty good sign you're not an Emotional Predator.

Make this book your own. Write all over it, make notes in the margins or create your own table of contents on the blank pages in the front or back of the book to help you quickly find sections that are particularly useful or relevant to your situation.

PART 1

◆ ◆ ◆

WHO AND WHAT EMOTIONAL PREDATORS ARE -
A NEW PARADIGM FOR UNDERSTANDING PROBLEM PEOPLE

Predator:

1) an animal that preys on others,

2) *a person who exploits others.*

chapter one

The True Nature of the Problem

"Beware of false prophets, who come to you in sheep's clothing,
but inwardly are ravenous wolves."
Matthew 7:15

What is an Emotional Predator? It's a person who exploits other people by manipulating them and preying on their emotions, and does this without restraint from conscience or the negative impact on others of their own toxic behaviors. They come in all shapes, sizes, genders, races, religions, and nationalities. And they are hidden among us.

Let's start by looking at an example of typical Emotional Predator behavior that includes omitting relevant facts to hide the truth, ignoring rules, denying facts, being indignant and bullying when called on bad behavior, blaming their target, being hypocritical, refusing to inconvenience themselves or change, being indifferent to their negative impact on others, playing the victim, and manipulating emotions with melodramatic tones and words.

At a mother's insistence, a court ordered that each parent could take only a seven day summer vacation with their four year old daughter, limiting her time away from either parent. The mother then scheduled to take nine days (ignoring rules when it suits them, even rules they previously insisted on, is common for Emotional Predators). When the father objected, this mother first denied she was taking more than seven days (denying plain facts is common Emotional Predator behavior). Then she got indignant and angry when the father spelled out the simple math that added up to nine days (getting indignant and angry when their own bad acts are exposed is a form of bullying and blaming their target that Emotional Predators often use). Finally, rather than change her plans and abide by the Court Order she had insisted on (hypocrisy is common in Emotional Predators), the mother told the father he also could take nine days, even though seven day vacations would have been better for her child (refusing to inconvenience themselves or change what they want, and being oblivious or indifferent to the negative impact on others, is typical of Emotional Predators).

But the most treacherous part of this incident is how the mother followed up a few weeks later by playing the "victim" of the father, telling her daughter *selected* true things, but *completely reversing the meaning of events by leaving out the relevant facts*. Here's how she lied by omission to reverse reality for her four year old. After the mother had taken her nine day vacation, when she dropped her daughter at her father's house for the nine day vacation with him, the mother told her daughter it was "sad" that the father was "going to keep you away from mommy for an extra long time now - because your father *thinks* I took extra days." With a melodramatic display of sadness in her words and tone, the mother led her daughter to believe that the father was wrong and bad for keeping mother and daughter apart for an extra long time because of what the father "thought." The daughter came into the father's house upset with the father for being unfair to the mother and mean to the daughter. The father had to slowly and clearly count days on a calendar and read his daughter the words of the Court Order and the emails with the mother that showed the full story of what the mother had done, which she was now blaming on the father.

The mother's story to the daughter was true, as far as it went. The father did in fact "think" the mother had taken extra days. But the mother's story left off the crucial fact that what the father "thought" also was *correct:* the mother *had* taken extra days. And it left off the fact that the mother had violated the rules she herself had insisted on and had done so over the father's objection.

As we all feel when we reconnect with reality, the child was relieved to understand the full truth from the calendar and documents: that she was now spending extra time with the father because of the mother's selfish, rule-breaking, hypocritical actions, not because the father's thinking was incorrect and not because the father was being unfair. The mother's innuendo, based on partial truth, that the father was victimizing the mother and daughter *was a complete reversal of the truth*. The mother's behavior was standard, unexceptional Emotional Predator conduct. It illustrates how an Emotional Predator will combine many tactics to use, abuse and manipulate others, even her own children, to get what she wants.

We live in a time of subtle danger. Selfishness and manipulation seem to be on the rise, while empathy seems to be disappearing. It's more important than ever for people of good heart and intention to learn to protect ourselves. To protect ourselves, we first have to recognize the problem, even if that means looking at some dark things. In my experience, it's more dangerous to ignore harsh realities than to face them. Danger presents opportunity.

If you've been confounded by a difficult person and the profession al help you've sought - perhaps from highly regarded and expensive experts - hasn't really changed much or anything at all, if the same pain in the butt person is inflicting the same pain in your butt perhaps for years now, and no advice or interventions have yielded more than temporary relief followed by a resumption of the same terrorizing behaviors, it may be because *our culture and many of the experts who are embedded within it don't understand the true nature of the most damaging hidden social problem we face today.* This book offers a radically different view of the problem people in your life and of human nature, and provides practical effective solutions.

There are predators hidden among us. They prey on us. They exploit us. These predators target unsuspecting decent people, wreaking havoc with nearly every aspect of their lives. These predators feed on the emotions of others, consuming their time, energy, money and well-being in the process. That's why I call them Emotional Predators.

The Merriam-Webster dictionary defines a predator as "a person who looks for other people in order to use, control, or harm them in some way." The Oxford dictionary defines a predator as "a person or group that ruthlessly exploits others." By all definitions, not a pleasant bunch.

By its nature, a predator doesn't stop to think of its prey. A predator isn't concerned with how its prey feels or what it suffers. A predator is one hundred percent occupied with getting what the predator wants - with feeding on its prey. Animal predators literally eat their prey. Emotional Predators will figuratively feed on you, draining your life energy, money, sleep, peace of mind, confidence - everything that nurtures a full and rich life.

One difficult thing to consider at the outset is that *the Emotional Predators that this book describes are not people like the rest of us.* They have human bodies, but their brains are different. They look like the rest of us, but inside their minds they are not like us in crucial ways. Most people live by rules of decency, common sense and respect for others; these decent people don't want others to suffer and they try to treat others the way they themselves would like to be treated. But the Emotional Predators among us do *not* live by those rules. Emotional Predators target these decent people. Good, naive folks who don't recognize Emotional Predators, often because they believe that all people are basically good, are Emotional Predators' easiest prey. This book can help you avoid becoming Emotional Predators' prey.

The most dangerous predators in nature hunt by *stealth* and camouflage, like lions crouching in tall grass to stalk antelope or ancient hunters wrapping themselves in animal skins to sneak up on a herd. These hunters are invisible to their prey until it's too late. *The human appearance of Emotional Predators is a disguise that lets them infiltrate and hide in every part of our world, making them particularly dangerous.* Like a big cat crouching low in tall grass, Emotional Predators hide in the busy activities of society and the shallows of social media, stalking their prey, learning about their prey's emotional weaknesses and vulnerabilities until they strike with the speed and agility of the fiercest carnivore. And then they consume the money, time, energy and emotional well-being of their targets. Fortunately, sometimes we notice the jerks, users, abusers, manipulators and pains-in-the-butt in our world. When we notice them, we can take steps to avoid them and limit their damage. But Emotional Predators work hard to stay hidden to catch their targets unaware. Emotional Predators look like normal people, they imitate normal people, they hide among normal people, *but they are fundamentally different.*

You may have seen the chaos Emotional Predators leave in their wake: the derailed hopes, the traumatized and stressed survivors of their attacks, the divorces, the custody fights, the business power struggles, the financial ruin, the needless litigation, the governmental gridlock. You may have suffered these traumas yourself. Emotional Predators lurk in every part of our society. The sensational cases that make the news, rare cases where they resorted to violence to feel powerful and dominant, catch our attention. But to see the scope of the problem, we need to refine our vision. Consider that *if there is significant recurring unnecessary conflict in a relationship, it usually means one or both people are Emotional Predators*, with serious mental illness - and this reality may well go unnoticed and unnamed. As we'll see later in this Chapter, Emotional Predators suffer from a range of mental illness diagnoses. But it's the suffering they cause others, and how to avoid it, that is our focus.

What are Emotional Predators after? *They relentlessly crave feeling themselves dominate, win, control and be the "puppet master." For Emotional Predators, life is a strategy game and other people are either players to be defeated or game pieces to be used.* Along the way, they'll consume anything and everything in their path. They might like money, houses, cars, prestige, authority and stuff, but those are only markers and implements to them of their power and dominance. And if you are in their path, they'll take your emotional life blood and well-being. Like the big cats, they have absolutely no concern for their prey. If they target you, you exist to them as something to be used.

Emotional Predators likely have been with our species from the start, and the history of humanity could be seen as a struggle to impose decency on our more base instincts of predation. Or it could be seen simply as the age old struggle against evil. Because we live in unique times under unprecedented threat of cataclysmic destruction and with communication devices that make predation easier, it's more urgent than ever that we understand the destructive impact of Emotional Predators in ways that offer genuine protection. Unfortunately, *current popular theories about human nature, grounded in psychoanalysis and psycho-dynamic psychology, are not up to the task.* The useful guidance these theories offer for solving problems with neurotic people does not work with Emotional Predators, and an emerging, broader paradigm for understanding human nature and difficult people is not yet widely understood. The nature of today's serious interpersonal conflicts is categorically different from what today's standard theories account for.

Let's look into these things a little more closely. As you read on, please bear in mind that new ideas that challenge deeply held beliefs can make us uncomfortable. I urge you to keep an open mind and consider that *fundamental things you have always known about other people may not be true.*

CURRENT POPULAR THEORIES ARE INADEQUATE

"Many of our ideas have been formed, not to meet the circumstances of this century, but to cope with the circumstances of previous centuries. But our minds are still hypnotized by them, and we have to dis-enthrall ourselves of some of them. ... It's very hard to know what it is you take for granted. And the reason is that you take it for granted."
Sir Ken Robinson (2010 TED talk)

The most pressing problems between people that many of us face today are not well understood by current popular theories of psychology and approaches to mental health, or by the society in general. Emotional Predators are not like the rest of us, and the rest of us make a fatal error in assuming that all people are more or less alike. Whether considering our personal or work relationships or the society as a whole, it's useful to understand the broad outline of the problem Emotional Predators present and how our assumptions about human nature and mental health are outdated. Just as one shoe size doesn't fit all feet, one approach to human relations doesn't fit all people either.

Our present assumptions about the psychology of difficult people are rooted in psychoanalytic ideas from the beginning of the twentieth century that emerged out of the end of the Victorian era (1837 - 1901). The Victorian era was a time of repression (pushing uncomfortable feelings out of awareness) that led to neurotic troubles. Its motto might be summed up as "don't even think about it." But, for decades, we've been living in a different, more indulgent time whose motto might be summed up as "just do it." This promotes what some now call character or personality disturbances, which are quite different from neurotic problems. I call people with these modern disturbances, Emotional Predators.

When I speak of neurotic people, I mean people who can become better people by gaining insight and understanding about themselves. Neurotic people can be well-adjusted, wonderful people or very troubled and troubling, but they are entirely different from Emotional Predators. Even the most well-adjusted healthy people I know are at least a bit neurotic, but by cultivating self-awareness their neuroses don't have a significant negative impact on them or others. Emotional Predators are too blinded by their own light to see any insights that would make them better people. *If an Emotional Predator gains any insight into himself, he will use it to become a worse person, to manipulate others more effectively for his own ends.*

Sadly, the self-serving tactics and attitudes of the problem people described in this book seem to have become more widely accepted, even encouraged, in our culture, particularly over the last half century or so. As this happens, we encounter Emotional Predators more often and it begins to look like an epidemic - an epidemic characterized by the disappearance of empathy. As we shall see in Chapter 2, a lack of empathy is a defining characteristic of Emotional Predators. A recent University of Michigan study found a forty percent decline in empathy among college students, with most of the decline taking place after 2000.[1] The study's author concluded that the current generation of college students, the so-called 'Generation Me', is "one of the most self-centered, narcissistic, competitive, confident and individualistic in recent history." By one estimate, a quarter of Americans have little or no empathy. Declining empathy may be why the Center for Disease Control also recently reported a twenty five percent increase in suicides over the same period across all demographics in the United States. But hopefully, as public awareness of the dangers and traits of Emotional Predators increases, new social norms will emerge that expose and condemn, rather than condone (or even reward), these destructive people. Our society as a whole will become more empathetic and compassionate.

As Western society has become more permissive and self-indulgent, Emotional Predators have become more numerous, contributing to social polarization and political gridlock. In 2001, Harvard professor Martha Stout estimated that four percent of the United States population were sociopaths. That is one out of every twenty-five people. If correct, that would mean there are over twelve million sociopaths in the United States. If your child is in a public elementary school with twenty five to thirty children in each class, and we assume each child has two parents, that's fifty to sixty parents per classroom. According to Dr. Stout then, the odds are that there are two sociopaths among the class parents. What Dr. Stout calls "sociopaths" are only one type of Emotional Predator. In my view, between ten and twenty percent, maybe more, of the adults in the United States are Emotional Predators.

Mental health professions (along with the legal profession, the courts and our society as a whole) are not currently equipped to handle the epidemic of Emotional Predators we face. In the introduction to his book, *Character Disturbance: The Phenomenon of Our Age,* Dr. George Simon explains the problem this way:

> "Many mental health professionals not only are trained primarily in classical theories of human behavior, but also cling to beliefs about human nature and the underpinnings of psycho-social dysfunction that originally emanated from these theories. For this reason, they often attempt to use the tenets and the principles that flow from more traditional paradigms to guide them in their efforts to solve today's very different kinds of psychological problems. In short, they attempt to understand and treat character disturbance with approaches and methods originally designed to treat extreme levels of neurosis.
>
> *... character disturbance is one of the most pressing psychological realities of our age; it's becoming increasingly prevalent; and it's an entirely different phenomenon from neurosis, requiring a*

different perspective to adequately understand and treat. (emphasis in original) ... It's important to recognize that disturbed characters differ dramatically from neurotics on almost every imaginable dimension of interpersonal functioning. They don't hold the same values, believe the same things, harbor the same attitudes, think the same way, or behave in the same manner as neurotics."

I applaud Dr. Simon for challenging "longstanding notions and deeply-held beliefs about why people experience psychological problems in the first place, and how professionals must assist them," and I join him in asking you to "accept the reality that our very different times have spawned problems the major helping professions have only recently begun to face [so that] you'll be better prepared to understand and deal with" Emotional Predators (Dr. Simon calls them character disturbed people).

Today, many experts and the society as a whole haven't caught up with our most pressing psychological and behavioral problems. Tackling the problem of Emotional Predators calls for a radical expansion of our understanding of the types of people that exist. To protect yourself, you must start by taking seriously the idea that *some people are nothing at all like the kind of person you are and are completely alien to you. They play by entirely different rules – rules that you can hardly believe possible. They have emotional responses, attitudes and behaviors that are almost inconceivably foreign to your own. These people, these Emotional Predators, lack everything you assume is at the core of human nature.*

DON'T BE DISTRACTED BY DIFFERENT LABELS AND DIAGNOSES

Emotional Predators have been called many things: Character Disturbed, Personality Disordered, Narcissists, Sociopaths, Psychopaths, Borderlines, Hysterics, Narcissistic Sociopaths, Sociopathic Narcissists, Malignant Personalities, Malignant Narcissists, Toxic Personalities and Covert-Aggressive Manipulators (among other things). Less technically, you may have heard people with these problems called users, abusers, manipulators, difficult people or just plain jerks. A neighbor of mine described his ex-wife as a "very slick hustler, the consummate con-artist." Just as a rose by any other name is still a rose, a turd by any other name is still a turd.

If you focus on their impact on others, you might describe Emotional Predators as Malignant Personalities. If you focus on the tactics they use, you might describe Emotional Predators as Covert-Aggressive Manipulators. If you're making a mental health diagnosis, you would choose a type of Personality Disorder: Narcissist, Sociopathic, Borderline, etc.... If you focus on their moral failings, you might describe Emotional Predators as Character Disturbed. But if you want to protect yourself from them, it's best to call them by how they behave, the ways they think and react, and how they impact others. And they behave, think, react and impact others like Emotional Predators, using (mostly covert) aggressive emotional manipulation in a malignant way, lacking the restraints of a mature, decent person of conscience.

In the language of mental health diagnoses, each Emotional Predator has her own particular mix of the features of five personality disordered types - sociopathic, narcissistic, hysterical, borderline and paranoid - with paranoid, sociopathic and narcissistic features prominent in all of them. Sociopathic types are more cold blooded and calculating manipulators. They strategize to get what they want in the most ruthless and chilling ways. Narcissistic types are more relentlessly focused on themselves and their image. They see only themselves and what they want. Hysterical types are drama queens and kings, making big emotional drama out of situations that would be quickly and calmly resolved by a mature person. Borderline types flip/flop and reverse themselves without even noticing. They are blatant hypocrites, consistently inconsistent. The only thing you can count on with borderline types is that you can't count on them. Paranoid types take as given that others are out to get them. Emotional Predators of all types are usually paranoid because they're constantly deceiving and conspiring to take advantage, so they assume everyone else is doing that to them. And all Emotional Predators are narcissistic to the extent that they pursue what they want at the expense of others, and sociopathic to the extent that they manipulate. *But every Emotional Predator is a mixture of these five personality disorder features.*

All of the people with these personality features, regardless of the mix of features, are Emotional Predators, continually manipulating with no concern for the costs to others, and no conscience or compassion. They all use, abuse and manipulate others without remorse. They want what they want. They want it now. To get it, they will do whatever they think they can get away with. And they hide their true nature and what they're up to. Most of them *at first* appear as charming, wonderful people. The less they are seen for what they really are, the more dangerous they are.

Regardless of the label we use, a fundamental underlying attribute that distinguishes Emotional Predators is their *missing conscience* and *incapacity for compassion,* both stemming from their *lack of empathy.* Chapter 2 explains this.

NAIVE VIEWS SET YOU UP TO BE A TARGET

Without knowing any better, a person of good conscience struggling with an Emotional Predator often will naively keep falling back on techniques for helping neurotic people. But approaches that can help when dealing with neurotics do not work with Emotional Predators. While Emotional Predators lack conscience, neurotics are handcuffed by too much conscience. While Emotional Predators are too self-focused, their neurotic targets aren't focused enough on themselves. Emotional Predators want to do what gets them power and advantage. Neurotic people want to do what's right for others, often at their own expense.

Emotional Predators know how good people operate and use it to their own advantage, exploiting a good person's predictable, empathy based other-focused responses. For example, playing on a good person's guilt is a favorite and easy tactic of manipulation. Emotional Predators know that good-hearted people will respond to others with conscience and a desire to help (or at least not harm). These are things an Emotional Predator does not do, but will exploit, for example, by playing the "victim." If you are good-hearted, to protect yourself you have to accept that *your natural responses - responses that flow from values you share with people of ample empathy and good conscience - can be counter-productive when dealing with an Emotional Predator.* Part 2 explains this more.

Some popular views held by good-hearted people can be dangerously naive when applied to Emotional Predators. One such view is that compromising is always the right thing to do. *There are no compromises with an Emotional Predator, there is only giving in to avoid conflict.* To get along with an Emotional Predator, you have to agree with her and give her everything she wants, when she wants it and how she wants it - even if what she wants is the opposite of what she wanted moments before. What you think is a compromise, is only you giving in, accommodating, backing down. Giving in *can* be a smart strategy, *if* you know what you're doing and why. In Part 2, we explore how to pick your battles wisely and yield on non-essential things.

When you "compromise" with an Emotional Predator, you think she'll reciprocate, but she never will. You think she'll appreciate your sacrifice - what it means to you, how it impacts you - but she never will. And, if you want to get along with her, you can't point out these things to her, or try to make her care about her negative impact on you. An Emotional Predator won't take in any information that she doesn't want to know. Her unfairness and selfishness, her requirement that she get her own way if you want to get along with her, and her one-way street approach are things she can't see the way a blind person can't see street signs. So, *if you believe that a good person always avoids conflict by being reasonable and compromising, and if you naively expect reciprocity and understanding from an Emotional Predator, you are an attractive target for Emotional Predators.* To put it another way, to an Emotional Predator, if you believe those things, you're a sucker.

Another popular view held by good-hearted people that can be dangerously naive when applied to Emotional Predators is that good people always treat all people equally, decently and with empathy and compassion. I've had good-hearted people ask me, "If empathy and compassion are good things, then shouldn't I give them to my abuser?" Sadly, the answer is *Not if you want to end the abuse.*

Briefly, some of the other dangerous beliefs you may hold about how to make things better with an Emotional Predator include: believing that you need to *understand why* a manipulative person is the way they are (better intellectual understanding); believing that you need to *give them more empathy* (better emotional understanding); believing that you need to *be more patient or try harder* (better mentoring); and believing that you need to *grow and develop yourself* into a better person (better personal growth). Lacking alternatives, many decent people cling to these beliefs about how to reduce relational problems, although none of them will help with an Emotional Predator. *With an Emotional Predator, no good deed goes unpunished.* All of these beliefs share the naive and mistaken view that the trouble with an Emotional Predator can be fixed if the *target* becomes a better person *toward and for* the Emotional Predator. *In fact, the target of an Emotional Predator needs to be better at protecting and caring for herself, not at doing anything for the Emotional Predator.*

Analyzing or Trying to Change Them Will Not Help

One of the approaches for neurotics that does not work with Emotional Predators is treating them as if they were like you and trying to understand their *unconscious* motivations. Psychoanalytic thinking assumes that coming to understand previously unknown aspects of ourselves, particularly our unconscious motivations, resolves problems and changes us. A natural early reaction to an Emotional Predator is to puzzle over *why* he is like that in order to know how he can be fixed. Good people want to *understand* Emotional Predators and *help* them. *But while a good person is distracted, puzzling over 'Why is he like that?', the Emotional Predator is busy scheming to mislead and take advantage.*

Why Emotional Predators are the way they are is an academic question that smart people have grappled with.[2] To summarize that work, both nature and nurture may contribute. Recent studies have shown that people are born with certain personality traits and temperaments which were correlated with different lengths of certain neurons at birth. That's not to say environment doesn't have a significant effect on how those traits and temperaments develop, socialize and express over a lifetime. The emphasis in Asian cultures on the collective over the individual seems to have a restraining influence on people with sociopathic natures. These are puzzles for a different book.

For the immediate purpose of protecting yourself right now, it's vital to realize that trying to understand the *cause - the "why" -* as the psychoanalytic paradigm wants to do, won't protect you. It's enough to recognize *how* they operate. When society and mental health professionals misunderstand the manipulative and malignant nature of Emotional Predators and how they operate in our world, society and mental health professions contribute to an environment that enables (and perhaps even nurtures) the anti-social behaviors of Emotional Predators. By misdirecting our efforts toward understanding Emotional Predators (rather than *recognizing* them and protecting ourselves), we inadvertently spoil, indulge and tolerate their aberrant behaviors, which provides them with rich feeding grounds - and their numbers swell.

Instead, think of an Emotional Predator as a land mine in the sunlit fields of your life. It would be irrelevant - and an unhelpful distraction - to ask whether a land mine knows what it's doing or is just unaware. That line of inquiry with Emotional Predators invites you to feel guilt for not understanding them well enough and to offer compassion toward them, both things they prey on. *Turning your attention instead to what Emotional Predators do – to how they operate – doesn't make you a bad person. It makes you a shrewd and effective defender of yourself and your loved ones. It empowers and protects you and your loved ones.*

Given the operative psychoanalytic paradigm of our culture, it's understandable if we find ourselves wanting to figure out why Emotional Predators are the way they are as a way of trying to change who they are. But trying to *change* an Emotional Predator's nature also won't protect you. Those efforts will waste your vital defensive energies and make you more vulnerable. Later on, we'll look at ways to change an Emotional Predator's *behaviors*, but don't confuse that with changing who they *are*, their intrinsic nature. You don't try to change a land mine into a flower. You recognize it and its danger, locate it in its hiding place, and get out of the way and/or disarm it (which involves armoring up yourself with impenetrable layers). After you're safe from land mines, you can plant flowers. For protection right now, understand *how* land mines operate, not *why*. It's enough to see that they operate by releasing a pin when you step on them which blows up an explosive. Understanding the chemistry of the explosives and the metallurgy of the case and trigger are different, longer term inquiries best left to specialists in the safety of the laboratory, after the fields of your life have been cleared of mines. Keeping yourself and your loved ones safe is enough of a challenge.

In the long term, let's hope science will discover new ways to disarm Emotional Predators. Geneticists may someday be able to repair genetic mutations. Social scientists may someday be able to prescribe corrective social and parenting environments. Pharmacology may someday produce a wonder drug to turn Emotional Predators into altruists. But, along with the rest of us, researchers doing that work first need to be immunized from the attacks of Emotional Predators. For now, it's enough - and vitally important - to recognize Emotional Predators' abusive behaviors and states of mind, and protect ourselves.

Emotional Predators are extremely dangerous in a direct and immediate way, and to protect yourself you have to always treat them that way. To protect yourself in the here and now, know how they operate and what they do, but don't be distracted by seeking underlying causes of why they are as they are or by trying to change them. And again, while changing their *behaviors* may be possible, don't confuse that with changing *who they are.*

TRADITIONAL THERAPY APPROACHES FOR NEUROTICS WILL NOT PROTECT YOU

Traditional therapy approaches that help *neurotic* people make things worse with Emotional Predators. Competent therapists using today's methods rooted in psychoanalytic concepts can help neurotic people who lack self-confidence and self-awareness (but have ample empathy, conscience and capacity for insight into themselves) become more authentically themselves, understand their unconscious motivations and be self-actualized. As neurotic people become more self-aware and self-actualized, they generally find the quality of their lives improve; they find a better job or career, attract a better mate, feel less anxious or depressed, overcome addictions and other self-destructive behaviors, and get more from their work and relationships. With neurotic problems, giving more empathy, understanding and patience, fostering more self-awareness and increasing personal growth are helpful. This is true whether you're dealing with your own neurosis, another neurotic person or the relationship between two neurotics. But these approaches have little use when you're dealing with an Emotional Predator.

Take, for example, increasing your own personal growth as a way to solve problems between people. This often includes instructions like "be who you are," "share your truth," "be authentic," and "don't be afraid to share your feelings and perceptions." Unfortunately, these types of personal growth approaches can be destructive when divorcing, or dealing in any capacity with, a high-conflict personality like an Emotional Predator. When you follow these approaches with an Emotional Predator, *he simply uses your candor to gather information he can use to manipulate you.*

An Emotional Predator uses traditional therapy to learn more sophisticated ways to *sound* sincere while manipulating. For example, in couples therapy, an Emotional Predator will learn to pledge to being "fully committed" to the relationship, but for him this means being committed to getting as much as possible *for himself* while giving as little as possible, because that's what "relationship" means to him. When that one-way street ends, he'll leave in a smoke screen of psycho-babble justifications. Emotional Predators can only commit to themselves and getting what they want. More than a few of them study psychology and become therapists to stock their manipulative toolbox with sophisticated ways to learn about other peoples' emotional vulnerabilities.

A therapist or other professional working with a client whose current or former spouse is an Emotional Predator, or who is dealing with a friend, family member or anyone else who's an Emotional

Predator, needs to *invert* the goal of traditional therapy for neurosis. *Instead of encouraging that client to be authentic and honest, the helping professional needs to counsel her to be strategic. Expressing one's true feelings, admitting vulnerability, and sharing insights into oneself can bury a person who's dealing in any capacity with an Emotional Predator* - especially when children are involved. And being strategic in itself doesn't make you a bad person. So screen professional helpers well, and only use those who you know can spot and truly understand Emotional Predators. Later in this chapter, I'll share an example of a psychologist who had an impressive resume and a convincing sales pitch about his ability to handle personality disordered people, but actually didn't have a clue when it came to managing an Emotional Predator.

THE GOLDEN RULE DOES NOT WORK WITH EMOTIONAL PREDATORS

"Respect on its own is cold and inert, insufficient to overcome the bad tendencies that lead human beings to tyrannize over one another."
Martha Nussbaum

In addition to misguided attempts to understand Emotional Predators and fix the problem with one's own personal growth, a well-intentioned person might try to treat them the way all decent people would like to be treated: with compassion, generosity, self-sacrifice, consideration, etc... That would be naive and dangerous. The Golden Rule - treat others the way you would like to be treated - would be a wonderful way to deal with everyone in an *ideal* world that, unfortunately, does not exist. It doesn't matter whether you state the Golden Rule in terms of action (compassion) - to treat others the way you would like to be treated - or in terms of restraint (conscience) - to not do to others what you would not want done to you. *Applying the Golden Rule to Emotional Predators makes you a patsy and an easy target, because Emotional Predators are not playing by that rule and they take advantage of those who do.*

If you treat an Emotional Predator the way you'd like to be treated, they'll walk all over you. To protect yourself, you often need to take a few pages from the Emotional Predator's play book and apply them strategically. Sometimes it's necessary to treat them the way they treat you, not the way you'd like to be treated. Being strategic about Emotional Predators doesn't make you an Emotional Predator.[3] The Golden Rule is an ideal vision of how humanity *should be*. It's dangerous to pretend that this is how humanity *actually is*.

Similarly, books like Robert Fulgham's delightful *What I Need to Know I Learned in Kindergarten* offer other romantic, but naive, approaches to living in a world that includes Emotional Predators. Fulgham suggests that adults should follow the basic rules of good behavior taught in Kindergarten. "Everything you need to know is in there somewhere. The Golden Rule and love and basic sanitation. Ecology and politics and equality and sane living." Fulgham's list includes things like being honest, sharing everything, and playing fair. These ideas are wonderful for a world of only well-meaning neurotic people, which doesn't exist. But they're dangerous for the world that includes Emotional Predators, which we live in. Put another way, Fulgham's advice about kindergarten lessons is well-intentioned, but incomplete. It offers a beautiful idealistic vision of how to live that leaves out the essential element of how to *safely* live in a world with evil.

Accommodating and treating Emotional Predators as you'd like to be treated, or making excuses or exceptions for their behavior, will make things worse. Treating an Emotional Predator with uncensored honesty and trust just gives her the information about you - about what's dear to your heart - that she needs to manipulate you. Sharing with an Emotional Predator is a one way street - she'll take what you share and share nothing in return. Playing fair with an Emotional Predator gives her advantage over you because she's not limiting herself to only fair play, she's using dirty tricks.

Fulgham's approach and the Golden Rule are appealing ideals for an idealized world. They offer ways to be a good person *in a world of good people*. To the extent we're dealing with other good people, they remain wonderful guides. The problem is we don't inhabit an idealized world populated by *only* good people. *We inhabit a world with many bad people too, a world with evil.* Treating bad people differently from good people doesn't make you bad. It makes you smart. To summarize, Fulgham's book addressed the world we'd *like* to live in. This book addresses a dangerous aspect of the world we do, in fact, live in.

A common, naive belief among parents and educators today is that younger children should be sheltered from negative experience. These adults don't want to scare children by talking about bad people among us, leaving the children unaware and vulnerable later to Emotional Predator attacks. This popular parenting style of ignoring the darker side of humanity may reflect a romantic ideal of childhood as an idyllic period of ignorant bliss that should be protected from "adult" concerns. But this attitude condescends to children and raises immature, naive adults, making us all less safe. It deprives children of confidence and competence to deal with the more troublesome moments in life. It fails to respect children's intuition and wisdom about classmates and others who aren't safe. We don't help or protect a child when we override her instinct that something is off and dangerous about another child (or an adult) and, in the name of equality or promoting universal high self-esteem, we demand that she "must play with everyone." We make it worse when we accuse her of being "exclusionary" or "not peaceful" when, as the victim of hidden aggression, she walks away or stands up for herself. (In any event, children and adults don't need *high* self-esteem, they need *accurate* self-esteem. As George Carlin pointed out, sociopaths have high self-esteem.)

Evil exists: both intentional evil and the "banal evil" of ignorance and lack of courage. Building a future with less evil is vital work that starts with protecting good people from dangers we face right now. Before we can create a world where everyone can safely live by the Golden Rule and Fulgham's advice, we have to protect ourselves from (and survive the attacks of) those who aren't living by them. *The first step to protecting yourself and your loved ones is to recognize Emotional Predators for what they are* and not be deceived by their charming or misleading facades.

Even "Experts" Do Not Always Know

If you don't know what Emotional Predators are and how to spot them, you won't be able to protect yourself or recognize the helping professionals who don't understand them either. Although mental health professionals and lawyers may assure you otherwise if you ask them, *a surprising number of them do not understand the true nature of the modern character-based disturbances that Emotional Predators have.*

As a group, even more than lawyers, many mental health profession-als *think* they do, but they don't. And as we'll see later on, a shocking number of them are Emotional Predators.

I tried to refer a family to a respected, expensive psychologist with advanced psychoanalytic training (psychoanalytic theory is the root of the outdated paradigm that misunderstands the true nature of Emotional Predators). He assured me he knew how to handle mod-ern personality-based problems. But when the problem Emotional Predator parent contacted him, she easily manipulated him, even though I'd warned him and even though, as she started unleashing her manipulations on him, I pointed out to him how she was impos-ing her agenda and using him. Stuck in an outdated paradigm about human nature, he couldn't help.

How did this Emotional Predator impose her agenda and con-trol things with this psychologist? Her goal was to avoid having her son see this psychologist while *appearing* to comply with get-ting him the therapy that she'd demanded in court to impress the judge. Although she carried her cell phone with her all the time and promptly answered all calls she deemed important to her, she let the psychologist's calls go to voice mail. Then she'd call him back on his office land line phone late at night when she knew he wouldn't be there, leaving messages that didn't answer his previous messages.

From the start, she controlled the *way* they would communicate (voice-mail), carefully avoiding any opportunity for him to actually speak to her, leaving vague voice mails that didn't directly answer his simple question of what times she could schedule an appoint-ment. She frustrated his attempts at direct communication, success-fully putting off having her son see him, while maintaining the fa-cade that she was "following up" with him by leaving her soft-toned "concerned" but evasive voice messages. Even when he was told that he needed to call her out on her avoiding game, control how they communicated and document her behavior in writing, he kept going with the cycle of useless voice messages. He didn't know that public exposure is one of the things Emotional Predators hate and will do almost anything to avoid. He didn't set firm boundaries and control the timing and medium of their communications. He just didn't get it. She played him for a fool. The child got no help.

Please don't get me wrong, I don't expect perfection from professionals or anyone else. Even the most savvy professional well versed in the true nature of Emotional Predators and how to effectively spot and defend against them can occasionally be caught off guard. It's in the nature of Emotional Predators that they sneak under their target's radar. That's what they do. In his book, *Without Conscience*, Robert Hare, a leading authority on psychopaths, described being taken in by someone organizing a conference he spoke at.

Some years ago, I was taken in by an Emotional Predator with well concealed borderline, hysterical and narcissistic features. She accurately read my relaxed, informal style, and my desire to help and trust others, and presented an appealing facade of informality and neediness. I relaxed my normal boundary and provided services without first getting a written retainer contract. When my work was done, she disappeared without paying. (True to Emotional Predator form, I recently learned that she has enrolled in school to become a counselor.) She taught me that each new Emotional Predator you encounter presents a unique challenge, and that, with Emotional Predators, no good deed goes unpunished. And although I do my best to be vigilant, she won't be the last Emotional Predator to pull the wool over my eyes. So be gentle with yourself if you've been bamboozled and taken in by an Emotional Predator.

chapter two

The Difference Between Emotional Predators and Decent People

"All through the day: 'I me mine, I me mine, I me mine.'
All through the night: 'I me mine, I me mine, I me mine.'"
George Harrison

EMPATHY - THE FOUNDATION OF DECENCY

The first, and fatal, mistake decent people make is to assume all people are more or less like they are - that all people have more or less similar emotional responses and empathy. Looking for the best in others is wonderful as long as it doesn't blind you to the worst in others.

To understand what Emotional Predators are, we need to know a bit about empathy and its role in creating a conscience and compassion in decent people. *Emotional Predators are characterized, first and foremost, by their lack of empathy, conscience and compassion.* The absence of these three vital parts of all decent people makes Emotional Predators fundamentally different from decent people. It makes Emotional Predators indecent. *Conscience and compassion are not possible for people who lack empathy,* so let's first quickly look at empathy, before turning to conscience and compassion.

Empathy is an immediate automatic congruent emotional response to another person's emotional state. Empathy automatically *transfers* feelings. Empathy isn't the same as *sensitivity* to another's feelings. Emotional Predators can be very skilled at sensing and tuning into other people's feelings, but they do so only to gain information to use to manipulate. Emotional leverage is powerful and Emotional Predators use that lever expertly to prey on other people. That's why I call them *Emotional* Predators.

An Emotional Predator can "feel" another person's emotional state, but the predator's inner response will be *in*congruent. For example, an Emotional Predator may feel safe, secure, uplifted, and reassured by another's confusion or fear. If I walk into a room of friends who've just found out that one of their loved ones was killed in a car crash, my empathy would automatically adjust my mood to be in sync with the mood in the room. I'd have an immediate *congruent* emotional response. I wouldn't think of myself in that moment. As unthinkable as it may seem, an Emotional Predator in that situation primarily would be aware of how the feelings she's picking up will affect her, and what she can gain from that.

Emotional Predators can *fake* sympathy when necessary to fool you into believing they're your emotional ally. But Emotional Predators never feel *for you*. They feel you *for themselves*. They work ruthlessly and relentlessly for themselves, while they distort reality to create a positive public image and justify their attacks and manipulations. They always have their own wants and interests operating - sometimes intentionally, sometimes automatically, sometimes consciously and sometimes just out of their awareness.

Emotional Predators are not guided by shame and guilt, as neurotic people are. When an Emotional Predator does the right thing for someone else, it's not to avoid shame and guilt, but to *avoid looking bad to other people* which could interfere with the Emotional Predator getting what he wants. As we'll see in the next section, an Emotional Predator's *regret* over being ineffective for himself may look like guilt, and he may present it as guilt, but it's not. *Guilt is not the same as regret* that the impression an Emotional Predator left or the strategies he used didn't get him what he wants. For example, a convincing Emotional Predator who'd alienated his ex-wife with unsuccessful bullying told me in a most distressed voice that he was "so sorry that things turned out this way." But when I asked what he would do differently in the future to make things better for his ex-wife, he abruptly changed the subject.

Along with guilt and shame, Emotional Predators also lack humility. To have humility, a person must know that, except for random good fortune, they could be in another person's unfortunate situation: that "there, but for the grace of God, go I." Emotional Predators can *fake* humility when they want to create a disarming image, but they can't be sincerely humble. They think too highly of themselves.

Emotional Predators really are different from the rest of us. Studies of sociopaths (a subset of Emotional Predators) in prison for violent crimes show that their brains don't respond to emotions the way other people's brains do. These sociopaths had the same neurological response as normal people to emotionally bland words like "table" or "chair". But, whereas normal people have a markedly different neurological response to emotionally charged words like "love" or "kiss," a sociopath's neurological response to emotionally charged words is the same as it is to emotionally bland words. For a sociopath, "love" has the same bland emotional impact as "chair."[4] Other studies show that some people have more mirroring neurons, and some people fewer.[5]

Emotional Predators cultivate sensitivity to other people's feelings in order to get the data they need to formulate strategy to gain power. Knowing someone else's emotional state is a *tool* Emotional Predators use to manipulate and get what they want, part of a mental game they play to win. None of that is empathy.

To summarize about empathy, for normal people feelings are contagious, more contagious than thoughts and empathy is an immediate automatic congruent emotional response to another person's emotional state. If your empathy is functioning correctly, you feel other people's emotional states, and your own feelings change *to bring you in sync* with them. But s*ensitivity* to other people's feelings by itself isn't empathy. Emotional Predators can be extremely sensitive to other people's feelings, using that information for their own ends, while completely lacking empathy. Now, let's look at the crucial role of empathy in creating a *conscience* and *compassion*, traits an Emotional Predator also lacks - because conscience and compassion require empathy.

Conscience and Compassion - The Fruits of Empathy

Conscience and compassion both come from empathy and are essential elements of decency. Conscience is empathy restraining us from doing bad things. Compassion is empathy spurring us to do good things.

Conscience is the part of decent people that keeps them from doing (or sometimes just thinking about doing) bad things to other people. Conscience is a *restraint on bad acts* (and thoughts). Decent people feel shame and guilt when they do or think things that would be bad for others. To feel guilt or shame, we must first feel an emotional sample of what the other person would feel; in other words, we must have empathy. So our empathy prevents us from doing bad things to others because it creates feelings of guilt and shame when we sample another's suffering; this is called conscience.

When another person is suffering from something I've done, my empathy produces a congruent suffering in me. Sharing their suffering stimulates discomfort in my conscience. For example, if I commit perjury to send an innocent person to prison, my conscience would bother me. My conscience would bother me because my empathy would produce in me an *immediate automatic congruent emotional experience* of the innocent person's suffering, which would bring forth shame and guilt in me. These feelings would come forth as a natural expression of my humanity, not as something I do by choice. So my conscience motivates me to not cause suffering for others, if for no other reason than to avoid feeling ashamed and guilty. Empathy allows us to seriously ask ourselves "How would I feel if someone did that to me?". This is highly useful for society, some would say necessary for us to have a civil society at all.

But because an Emotional Predator doesn't get an emotional sample of another's feelings from empathy, he doesn't feel the discomfort of guilt or shame when he causes another person's suffering. He lacks guilt and shame; he has no conscience. Again, sensing another person's feelings and imagining how that person feels *as an intellectual exercise* in order to take advantage - or as a source of satisfaction - are not part of conscience. The lack of a conscience in Emotional Predators is one of their defining traits. Dr. Robert Hare's foundational book about psychopaths is titled *Without Conscience* for good reason.

Conscience is an internal restraint on evil. Where conscience fails, rules and laws take over as external restraints. But rules and laws can be manipulated by the unscrupulous and can even become instruments of evil. Slavery, racial and religious persecution, and even mass murder have all been carried out pursuant to laws. Except in extraordinary situations where their conscience demands otherwise, decent responsible people follow rules consistently. In contrast, even in ordinary situations Emotional Predators follow rules only when it benefits them, and they maneuver around rules as needed to abuse others. They'll encourage you to break rules when it serves them, and insist that you follow rules (resorting to shame, guilt, seduction and bullying) when that serves them. That kind of hypocrisy is standard operating procedure for an Emotional Predator.

Conscience is different from *calculated strategic self-gain*. Guilt and shame are different from *regret*. Emotional Predators can, and often do, regret not being effective in their manipulations and strategies, but they don't feel guilty or ashamed. They are driven only to get what they want and are constrained only by their perceived self-interest. If an Emotional Predator balks at doing something bad to someone else, it's because of the risk of negative consequences *to the Emotional Predator*. They never commit a selfless act of kindness or generosity. They're always looking out for themselves. If they can get away with it and it benefits them, they'll do it. If they don't get away with it or it doesn't get them what they want, they'll regret being *ineffective*. This is completely different from decent people avoiding the guilt and shame their conscience produces if they do bad things to others.

With respect to conscience, a psychopathic serial killer is similar to a ruthless corporate CEO or demagogue politician. "Chainsaw" Al Dunlop was a corporate CEO who gained notoriety for taking charge of companies and ruthlessly firing employees to reduce costs. He readily admitted he exhibited the traits of a psychopath.[6] Others act similarly, but are less candid. One could ask whether the poisoning of thousands of children for corporate profit is more evil than the murder of five random people. A person of conscience could do neither of these things. Some have said that Donald Trump exhibits traits of a Narcissist (which is another subset of Emotional Predator). I believe the co-author of his book, *The Art of the Deal* thinks he's a sociopath and has said he would now title the book "The Sociopath." Richard Nixon was widely believed to suffer a paranoid and narcissistic personality disorder. Many think Bill and Hillary Clinton are clever narcissistic manipulators.

A ruthless CEO and a demagogue politician pursue what they want without the restraint of empathy and conscience. One difference between a psychopath serial killer and a ruthless corporate CEO or politician is that the CEO and politician have more accurately calculated the risk/benefit *to themselves* within our society of what they do; they have assessed social reality more accurately and chart a more socially sanctioned path as a better way to get the experience of power and domination they relentlessly crave. None of these Emotional Predators is restrained by conscience.

While conscience is the part of decent people that keeps them from doing bad things to others, compassion is the part of decent people that drives them to do selfless good things for others. Compassion is a *spur to good acts*. When I do something good for someone else, my empathy brings me a taste of their pleasant experience which brings forth feelings of well-being and connection in me. This motivates me to provide positive experiences for others. And I try to provide experiences that'll be positive for the other person, not ones that I *think* they would like if they were me. This is how empathy moves us to be compassionate toward others.

Whether moving us to avoid the discomfort of shame and guilt through the restraint of conscience, or producing feelings of well-being through compassionate acts, empathy is an essential part of a mature, decent person. You could say that conscience and compassion require empathy as a bicycle requires wheels. Empathy puts a person in another person's shoes to feel what it's like to walk a mile in them. It's the basis for the Golden Rule. But, as we've seen, people of good conscience and compassion - decent people - put themselves in peril when they follow the Golden Rule with Emotional Predators, not realizing Emotional Predators can't reciprocate and will mistreat people who follow the Golden Rule with them.

Because they lack empathy, Emotional Predators can have neither conscience nor compassion. In this key respect, they are disturbingly different from decent people. Without conscience, they have no regard for the negative impact on others of what they do in their pursuit of what they want. Without compassion, they never do a selfless act; they always act only for their own gain.

CORE TRAITS AND BEHAVIORS OF AN EMOTIONAL PREDATOR

Let's take a quick look at some core traits and behaviors of Emotional Predators. In Part 2, as we learn ways to protect ourselves, we'll go over these traits and behaviors again in more detail. Don't forget that underlying all the traits and behaviors of Emotional Predators is the fact that, for them, other people's feelings are things to manipulate for their own gain.

Emotional Predators are relentlessly driven to dominate, win, control - to be the puppet master, jerking others around at the end of a string. In relationships, they always seek advantage over others and to use others to get what they want for themselves. They are not merely motivated this way. A person's motivations might be changed, if we could get through to them. *Emotional Predators' drive to dominate is a core and unchangeable part of who they are. It's their "prime directive," if you will, that they never violate.* The *ways* they seek to gratify their drive to dominate can change, but not the drive itself. If an Emotional Predator believes that he can control you by being nice, he'll be nice. If he believes he can control you by being a violent bully, he'll be a violent bully. But his underlying drive to feel power through control doesn't change.

Some Emotional Predators satisfy their need to feel powerful by creating unnecessary havoc, confusion and chaos, and watching you jump through meaningless hoops and navigate around needless road blocks they've thrown in your way. Many Emotional Predators naturally gravitate to positions of power where they can exercise power over others as part of their job, where they can hide under the cover of respected authority. And Emotional Predators can learn the rules of right and wrong, but they understand those ideas only as intellectual abstractions about how to play a game to win and defeat others, how to gain advantage and get what they want.

Emotional Predators spend a lot of energy managing their image and maintaining a false facade. It's a core activity for them. They're always monitoring how other people are seeing them. An Emotional Predator would rather *look* good than *be* good - and *being* good is different from being good *at* something. Being good is about conscience, compassion and social responsibility. Being good at something is about technique.

Emotional Predators are experts at faking sincerity and making emotional displays that influence others. They may flash anger to intimidate you into giving in, or get teary-eyed to elicit sympathy as a way of disarming you. Emotional Predators can hypnotize you into complying with their agenda with all the tricks of magicians - entertaining you, misdirecting your attention, showing what you want and expect to see - while they keep their real purpose hidden.

Emotional Predators use many tactics in addition to image management to hide what they are and do.[7] They play innocent. They play ignorant. They lie by leaving out relevant facts (lying by omission). They deny plain facts with bluff and lies (which is different from the *psychological* denial of emotionally uncomfortable things that neurotics do). They claim to be the victim needing your sympathy and help. They blame the people they are victimizing. They "gaslight" their targets. They isolate their targets. They are gifted debaters who make the better appear the worse and the worse appear the better. They assert the opposite of reality, with absolute, unquestionable authority and confidence - and because their universe truly is all about them, they believe their own BS, which can make them quite convincing. Sometimes they lie through their teeth for fun or profit. Either way, *an Emotional Predator's words can never be relied upon.*

Emotional Predators see their own disturbed traits in others. (This is called projection.) More insidiously, they *provoke* others to endure the inner turmoil that they can't handle within themselves. (This is called projective identification.) They're experts at passive aggression, withholding whatever a decent person would supply. They avoid giving direct answers to simple questions or requests. They stray off topic when the topic is their bad behaviors or anything else they don't want to address. They offer excuses and justifications, rather than change. They steadfastly resist complying with the rules of society or accommodating anyone else's needs. And they can be expert at subtly disrupting other people's natural rhythms.[8] All of these tactics and traits are described in detail in Chapter 3.

The Hidden Aspect – Concealed versus Visible Aggression

Emotional Predators operate most successfully when their operations are hidden from others. What you don't see can hurt you the most, so remaining invisible - stealth - is one of their core tactics. In the 1931 film *Dracula*, Professor Van Helsing the vampire slayer explained, "The strength of the vampire is that people will not believe in him." So it is with Emotional Predators. The strength of the Emotional Predator is that people will not believe that she really is what she is. Emotional Predators thrive in darkness, but they wither when exposed to the light of truth. The 1944 film *Gaslight* (with Ingrid Bergman, Charles Boyer, Joseph Cotten, Dame May Whitty, and Angela Lansbury) tells a classic tale of hidden abuse and overcoming it with the help of an outsider who illuminated the Emotional Predator's darkness with truth. It's worth watching more than once. Gaslighting is explained in Chapter 3.

Because Emotional Predators are aggressive, but in a hidden way, it's helpful to recognize the difference between aggression that is hidden (called covert) and aggression that is visible (called overt). Emotional Predators are masters of *covert* aggression, which is concealed and invisible. They hide their attacks, making them invisible to the uninformed observer. In contrast, the uninformed observer can usually recognize *overt* aggression, which is revealed and visible. So an Emotional Predator usually avoids overt aggression, *while at the same time provoking it from their target so the target looks like the problem*. Emotional Predators come in all shapes, sizes and styles, but the quiet gentle type can be particularly easy to miss because their aggression more easily hides behind that kind of facade.

Aggression also can be active or passive. Active aggression *delivers something negative to someone else*, like hitting or yelling or making a hurtful insult. It's almost always visible (overt). In contrast, passive aggression is *withholding or not doing something that would be positive for the other person*, like a response to a question or sex or information, or even a common courtesy. Passive aggression is invisible (covert), but not all invisible aggression is passive. For example, torture that leaves no marks and can't be heard is covert aggression that's active. The invisibility of all covert aggression makes it treacherous and intensely traumatizing and provoking to the target. Emotional Predators are expert at covert aggression, but they prefer the passive type because it's effortless and it's especially hard to see what's *not* done. But what's not done can be the essential truth of the matter and can be very hurtful.

Covert aggression is a central mechanism of *projective identification*. Projective identification is a process in which a disturbed person provokes and elicits within the target the negative feelings that the disturbed person can't tolerate within themselves. It's explained in detail in Chapter 6. The insipid thing about all covert aggression is that it almost always *provokes* an irritated, angry, depressed or anxious reaction, particularly when it's doled out in small doses over a long time. And when the target eventually runs out of patience and reacts, that *reaction* is overt and the only thing an uninformed observer notices. Once the Emotional Predator has provoked an overt reaction from her target, she points to her target's reaction to cast blame on her target, the true victim. *The reaction to abuse is seen and condemned while the covert abuse remains invisible.*

Sometimes emotional abuse can feel worse than physical abuse because others don't see it and that invisibility adds an extra layer of isolation to the hurt. A good example of this is a wife who refused to touch or be touched by her husband for a decade while she had several affairs. When he finally yelled at her about it, she blamed him to the world for what she called his "abusive" outburst. She twisted his single episode of yelling, which was overt and visible to others, into the "problem," ignoring her decade of hurtful passive aggression (withholding touch) and active covert aggression (her affairs), both of which were invisible to others. By leaving out of sight the relevant facts from which we would see the truth of the matter, *covert aggression is a treacherous form of lying by omission*. An Emotional Predator lies by omission when she tells selected true things, but reverses or distorts the meaning of events by leaving out the relevant facts, creating plausible emotionally compelling stories based on partial truth. Chapter 3 explains this.

Emotional Predators are a hidden threat, in part, because they're not playing by normal rules. In warfare, guerilla tactics depend on blending into the environment. When the United States "defeated" Saddam Hussain's army in Iraq, it didn't win. The other side just took off their uniforms and melted into the general population to resurface later as "insurgency" - peaceful citizen by day, attacker (or freedom fighter) by night. When you can't see who the aggressors are and what they're up to, they're harder to neutralize.

The 1957 horror film, *Invasion of the Body Snatchers*, presents a nice allegory for the hidden aspect of the threat posed by Emotional Predators. In the movie, aliens duplicated and replaced humans while the humans slept. (Emotional Predators attack us when we're unaware, or "asleep".) The impostor aliens looked like normal people on the surface, except that they lacked normal human emotions. (Emotional

Predators look like others, but they lack the normal human emotional response of empathy.) The invasion of these "pod people" aliens - they hatched from giant seed pods - was invisible to most people. (Most people don't see the Emotional Predators among us for what they are.) Pod people had certain characteristics by which they could be detected, such as the absence of a pulse and the inability to bleed or bend their pinky finger, but these traits were hard to detect in the normal course of things. (The heartlessness, covert-aggressive manipulations, lying by omission, and other tactics of Emotional Predators can be hard to notice.) Pod people needed to suck up huge amounts of psychic energy from normal people. (Emotional Predators wear you out and drain you dry.) Pod people's disguise as human replicas was the most frightening aspect of the movie. They just blended in and caught the real humans off guard. (In every part of nature, the better the camouflage, the more dangerous the predator. In our social world, a hidden problem is hard to avoid.)

The epidemic of Emotional Predators today is a bit like the invasion of the body snatchers by impostor pod people aliens in the movie. Emotional Predators and pod people both operate in secret. They look like everyone else, but lack essential elements of being fully human. They prey on humans. They serve their own ends at the expense of others. The rest of us are unaware of the danger.

Now that you're familiar with the unsettling nature of the dangerous and growing problem - the epidemic - of the Emotional Predators hidden in our world, you have a solid foundation for protecting yourself and your loved ones. Part 2 will give you the tools you need to build strong defenses on that foundation. A problem understood is a problem that can be solved, so take heart; you are well on the way to safety from the users, abusers and manipulators hidden among us.

PART 2

◆ ◆ ◆

HOW TO PROTECT YOURSELF FROM EMOTIONAL PREDATORS

"Recognizing a problem is an invitation to do something about it. ...
[I]t's much better to face harsh reality that to close our eyes to it. Once
you are aware of the dangers, your chances of survival are much better
if you take some risks than if you meekly follow the crowd. ... As long
as I can find a winning strategy, however tenuous, I don't give up. In
danger lies opportunity. It's always darkest before dawn."[9]
George Soros

INTRODUCTION TO PART 2

In Part 2, you'll learn specific ways to insulate yourself from Emotional Predators' abuse and manipulations. Those tactics and techniques are divided into five strategic steps:

Step 1, *Identify* Emotional Predators (Chapter 3)

Step 2, *Know yourself* better than they know you (Chapter 4)

Step 3, *Be Flexible* about how you define yourself (Chapter 5)

Step 4, *Avoid and Disengage* when possible (Chapter 6)

Step 5, *Be Strategic* when you do engage (Chapter 7).

Chapter 8 reviews. Chapter 9 offers some closing thoughts about contributing to a more decent world and some paradoxes.

A note about strategies and tactics: a *strategy* is a comprehensive guide - an approach - to solving a problem or managing a situation. It's a plan to achieve a long term goal. The strategies in this book are the five steps, covered in chapters 3 through 7. A *tactic* is a way to implement a strategy. A single tactic can be useful for implementing several different strategies. And a strategy may use a number of different tactics. Think of strategy as the guiding hand behind the selection and use of tactics.

While the five strategies for protecting yourself apply in all situations involving Emotional Predators, not every tactic in Part 2 will fit you and your situation. Some ideas may strike a chord and others may not seem to apply. But ideas that seem irrelevant now may be useful later on. So take what's useful now and adjust as you see what works and what doesn't.

There is no "one size fits all" approach to dealing with an Emotional Predator in your life. Each Emotional Predator is her own unique mix of the features described in Chapter 1: Sociopathic,

Narcissistic, Paranoid, Borderline and Hysterical. And each situation is unique. This means that no single strategy or tactic can be guaranteed to neutralize every Emotional Predator. Learning how to protect yourself is a process of *trial and error*. And trial and error doesn't work when we demand perfect results each time. So let yourself off the hook of perfectionism. When a tactic doesn't work as you'd hoped, it's not a failure, it's a learning opportunity.

Some of the ways to protect yourself can be easy to understand but difficult to put into practice and internalize, others harder to understand. Don't worry if you don't understand or remember everything right away. I'll repeat important points as we go, and you can revisit different sections as needed. Trust that you'll absorb what you need when and as you need it, using this book as a resource to refer back to, re-visiting different chapters from time to time. Make notes in the margins, on the Table of Contents or on the blank pages at the beginning or end. Create your own table of contents so you can find things that are particularly important to you.

chapter three

Step 1 - How to Identify Emotional Predators

The better the camouflage, the more dangerous the predator.

"His speech was smooth as butter, yet war was in his heart; his words were softer than oil, yet they were drawn swords."
Psalm 55:21

"Smiling faces sometimes pretend to be your friend. Smiling faces show no traces of the evil that lurks within. Smiling faces, smiling faces, sometimes they don't tell the truth."
Barrett Strong and Norman Whitfield

AN INITIAL CONCERN - HOW YOU ARE DIFFERENT

The first step in protecting yourself from Emotional Predators is to recognize them behind their camouflage. So in this Chapter 3, we'll look at common Emotional Predators behaviors, tactics and traits, their attitudes, and the professions they're attracted to - and some techniques for identifying those things in someone who may seem like a decent person but isn't.

As you read about the behaviors, tactics and traits of Emotional Predators, you may recognize some of them in yourself and worry that *you* may be one of them. We all can share some of the behaviors that distinguish Emotional Predators from others, and under stress we can temporarily regress to some of those more primitive ways (and many teenagers seem to temporarily regress that way as part of a natural developmental phase). And as we'll see, we also can choose to selectively adopt some Emotional Predator tactics to defend ourselves from Emotional Predators.

Emotional Predators exhibit a pervasive and enduring pattern of behavior and perception, not a selective, temporary use of tactics. That's why it can take repeated observations over time and examining documented history to determine whether someone is an Emotional Predator, or just a decent person temporarily regressed under stress or selectively resorting to defensive tactics.

You don't become an Emotional Predator by selectively using some of the clever or even devious Emotional Predator tactics to protect yourself and your loved ones. You can choose to use the same *tactics* without sharing the same *traits and nature*. Selectively playing an Emotional Predator's game better than she does in order to protect yourself, and with concern for the negative impact on innocent people, is very different from the Emotional Predator's pervasive use of tactics to use and abuse others for her own ends without regard to the costs imposed on others.

If you recognize Emotional Predator behaviors in yourself *and it troubles your conscience*, it means that you are not an Emotional Predator. Emotional Predators are distinguished by their lack of guilt and remorse for their impact on others. They lack the conscience which is necessary to produce guilt and remorse. Feeling bad about yourself and guilty over how you've treated others is nearly conclusive proof that you are not an Emotional Predator. As we saw in Part 1, *guilt* is not the same as *regret* over not being effective in getting what you want.

And Emotional Predators lack insight into themselves. They're deeply delusional about who they are and, in particular, how they impact others. Although they can fake it using the jargon of psychotherapy, they're not truly introspective. Recognizing Emotional Predator behaviors and tactics in yourself, suggests that you're more introspective than they are.

An Emotional Predator lacks empathy, conscience and introspection. You have all three. An Emotional Predator uses tactics offensively and relentlessly. You use them defensively and selectively.

EMOTIONAL PREDATOR BEHAVIORS, TACTICS AND TRAITS

Their Relentless Drive to Dominate, Control and Win

Although no two Emotional Predators are exactly alike, all Emotional Predators are relentlessly driven to dominate, control, and win, and pretty much everything they do is geared toward achieving those experiences. They need to feel like a powerful puppet master, jerking others around at the end of a string. In relationships, they always seek power and advantage over others and to use others to get what they want for themselves. They're not merely motivated this way. A person's motivations might be changed, if we could get through to them. *Emotional Predators' drive to dominate is a core and unchangeable part of who they are. It's their "prime directive," if you will, that they never violate.* The ways Emotional Predators seek to gratify their drive to dominate can change, but not the drive itself. Let's look at some of those ways.

Manipulating your emotions is a core tool - *the* core tool - of Emotional Predators, and they do this in many different ways. They play on your conscience, inviting you to feel guilty or ashamed when you've done nothing wrong, by pretending to be hurt or upset because of you. They bully and threaten you, using fear to control. Sometimes all it takes to intimidate a good person is to flash anger for a moment, especially when the anger comes from someone who's previously acted gentle and soft. Emotional Predators can abruptly shift their behavior to keep you off balance and as part of their all-or-nothing ways.

Some Emotional Predators satisfy their need to feel powerful by *creating unnecessary havoc, confusion and chaos,* and watching you jump through meaningless hoops and navigate around needless road blocks they've thrown in your way. They'll make a mountain out of a molehill just to watch you labor over or around it, and enjoy knowing they made you do that. Ironically, while Emotional Predators can be coldly rational planners, they remain irrational in the bigger picture because they don't recognize that good faith and cooperation would save everyone, including them, time, stress and money.

One way Emotional Predators try to dominate and control is to set up *"no-win" binds* for you, where you're damned if you do and damned if you don't. A no-win bind often takes the form of presenting a constantly moving target of demands, requirements or concerns for you to address. If you're a football fan, you can think of this as constantly moving the goal posts farther away to ensure a field-goal kicker's failure. Like the whack-a-mole game, as soon as you take care of one thing the Emotional Predator wants, he'll present another. Like Lucy pulling the football away each time Charlie Brown tires to kick it, he'll convince you to try again.

A woman married to an Emotional Predator could never satisfy him. When she had a good job in an office making good money, he complained that she wasn't home enough. When she quit that job to work from home buying, repairing and re-selling used clothing, he complained that she wasn't earning enough and she was always under foot. When she closed her re-selling business and took another high paying job in an office - you guessed it, he complained that she wasn't home enough. And his complaints were always couched as accusations that she was failing him or the family, or that she was just an all-around failure, which played to her overly sensitive guilt reactions.

Similarly, when a client's wife complained that their house was too small, he stretched his budget (she didn't work although she was a highly trained professional) and took on lots of economic stress to buy a bigger house for her. Within a month of moving in, she was complaining that the new house wasn't in a good enough location. When someone constantly complains that you're causing their unhappiness or failing them no matter how often you give them what they say they want, it's a good time to consider whether they might be an Emotional Predator setting up "no-win" binds for you.

Closely related to "no-win" binds is an Emotional Predator's habit of being *consistently inconsistent* as a way of dominating you by keeping you "always wrong." Being consistently inconsistent is a form of hypocrisy that provokes frustration, confusion and anger. Emotional Predators are hypocrites whose words and behaviors aren't congruent. One day they'll criticize you for giving your children maple syrup on their pancakes because sugar is bad for them. The next day they'll take the children for ice cream to buy their loyalty. And these inconsistent flip-flops and hypocrisies can happen in an instant. Believe it or not, an Emotional Predator could criticize you for giving the children "sugary" ketchup at dinner, while they're bringing out cake for dessert.

And if you point out her no-win binds or hypocrisy to the Emotional Predator, or don't give her whatever she demands in any given moment, she'll become difficult, angry and accusing, or offer up lame rationalizations, or completely ignore what you've said. The worst Emotional Predators will become violent, which is the most visible way of trying to dominate and control. In contrast, a decent person can change their mind without being a hypocrite. Decent people will acknowledge and apologize for the difficulties and frustration their change of heart caused for you, and changing their requests and positions won't be a regular pattern.

When you're the target of an Emotional Predator, you'll find yourself on a *one-way street*, with all efforts, energy and benefits going to them, but few or none returning. They will offer up endless justifications and excuses and reasons why they can't be there for you. And no matter how many times they let you down, they'll convincingly promise that next time will be different, and they'll blame you for the problems they create. If you don't know about Emotional Predators, you'll take responsibility and blame yourself. A classic statement of a good hearted but naive target is "if I just give a little more, try a little harder, be a little more patient and understanding, he'll treat me well."

Emotional Predators are *masters of deceptive and misleading stories*. They are sophists who twist words to make the worse appear the better and the better appear the worse. The lies they tell are designed to manipulate your emotions so you'll give them what they want. Their lies also cover up their true nature and behaviors with a charming and disarming facade. Often their deceits are designed to get others to see them as either a victim or hero. In our society, victims and heroes tend to get special accommodations and sympathy, which gives them power, so Emotional Predators love to play victim and hero. At the start of the book, I described an Emotional Predator who misled her young daughter by leaving out crucial facts to make it look like she and the daughter were the victims of the father. This mother left out the fact that the father's *thoughts* about the mother's vacation scheduling shenanigans were correct and she left out the fact that she had acted badly and created all the problems.

An Emotional Predator will *lie by omission*, telling plausible emotionally compelling stories based on partial truth to win sympathy and support, and to turn people against you. When they lie by omission, they leave out the context, facts and history that would provide a full and accurate understanding of things. They count on the reality that it's not always easy or practical to slow down and seek out the facts that they've left out. *Emotional Predators often communicate more through what they leave out than through what they include.* What they do *not* say can contain more useful information than what they say.

A divorced dad told me that at the time of the divorce, his ex-wife had "run off" to another state with their young children "to take them from me and cut them off from me." He said these things with the most convincing puppy dog victim eyes and soft, sad but slightly outraged tone. The clear message was how badly he'd been victimized and how horribly vindictive his ex-wife had been. About a month later when I met with his ex-wife, she showed me copies of police reports and letters from him that clearly documented his repeated acts of violence toward her and their children, and she mentioned that, on advice of the police, she'd taken the children to a domestic violence safe house in another state. This is a good example of why it pays to look behind plausible emotionally compelling stories and investigate the facts. What he'd presented as her "stealing" their children, turned out to have been her legitimate flight for safety from him. Until I saw the written independent documentation of the facts he'd left out, I was convinced the mother had treated the children as pawns in a divorce game of keep-away. Probing deeper, I found out that it was the father who regarded the children as pawns to use for his own ends, which revealed his accusations about the mother to be his projections. This Emotional Predator dad displayed lying by omission, projection and blaming the victim in just this one communication with me.

Related to lying, Emotional Predators will often mislead you by *diverting your attention* with too many or irrelevant details. Like a magician, when an Emotional Predator can get your attention on irrelevant things, you're less likely to notice what they're really up to. Again, whether lying or misdirecting your attention, what he doesn't say can reveal more than what he does say. You can notice this when you ask a direct question and he doesn't answer, although he offers up lots of words that are little more than distractions.

I asked a father to send me the police report that he'd told me described sexual abuse of his daughter by his ex-wife's new stepson. He sent me a long attention-grabbing email describing his daughter's traumatic reactions and behaviors, but no police report. I asked three more times for the police report and each time he sent me more inflammatory and dramatic descriptions of his daughter's anxiety and distress, but didn't send or mention a police report. In fact, there was no police report because his daughter hadn't been abused. He made up the distracting emotionally compelling abuse accusation and counted on me to take his word for it that a police report documented it. There was an element of truth in his lie. His daughter was anxious and distressed. That part of the story was true. But her anxiety and distress was being caused by the father's pressure to get her to lie to support his lies, all part of his scheme to take the daughter away from the mother, who was a great mom.

Most Emotional Predators are expert at using *non-verbal communication* to entertain, charm and seduce, and also to bully and intimidate, or elicit sympathy, when necessary. They can be *too* sincere, manipulating through body postures that convey committed interest, making a display of nodding their understanding, leaning in a little too assertively. And they can use body posture and gestures as a thinly or not so thinly veiled form of bullying. Some pundits thought Donald Trump did this to Hillary Clinton when he seemed to stalk around behind her during a 2016 presidential debate.

And Emotional Predators can be masters of *manipulating through eye contact*. An Emotional Predator may make eye contact that doesn't blink and hangs on a bit too long in order to convey sincere committed interest, "deep" connection, or vulnerability. A colleague described an arch manipulator who'd disarm others by crying on demand. I've seen Emotional Predators convey innocence and sincerity by opening their eyes so wide that you see white above and below their pupils at the same time. And that kind of eye contact can morph from convincing you of their sincerity into direct intimidation and aggression. Robert Hare interviewed psychopaths who readily admitted using a cold stare to intimidate by challenging others to meet their gaze without looking away. Subjected to that kind of staring attack, a good person can mistakenly believe that her discomfort reflects her own short coming, some lesser ability to "make contact."

One moment an Emotional Predator might offer you the sad eyes of blurry, tearful innocence. The next, those eyes could be boring into you with laser focused hostility. A woman on the witness stand in court kept a wide eyed "doe in the headlights" look for the judge. Then when the judge looked away, she shot her ex-husband daggers of vicious hatred with her eyes. Then she switched like a light back to doe-eyed innocence to meet the judge's eyes again. If you pay close attention when she doesn't know you're watching, *you can sometimes see in the eyes of an Emotional Predator both the angry wolf lurking within and the innocent vulnerable sheep facade.*

They are Devoted to Managing Their Image

Emotional Predators invest tremendous energy in managing their image. They'll say whatever they think they need to say to get someone to like them and give them what they want. They'll say different things to different people, being "politically correct" with whichever person they're with. To their National Rifle Association boss, they'll oppose gun control. To their pacifist girlfriend, they'll support gun control. *An Emotional Predator would rather look good than be good.* In contrast, decent people can be concerned with how they *look* to others, but decent people also will want to *be* genuinely good toward others. *Emotional Predators won't try to be genuinely good toward others, they'll try to be good at getting what they want. Decent people have conscience and social responsibility. Emotional Predators have technique.*

One way Emotional Predators hide their true nature is *appearing* to feel guilty or ashamed, saying all the right words of contrition and sorrow, when what they're really experiencing is just *regret* for not being effective for themselves. Don't be fooled. When an Emotional Predator says she's "truly sorry," she's sorry *that it didn't work for her or she got caught*, but she's not sorry for how you suffered because of what she did. Emotional Predators can be quite convincing, because they can be deeply sorry for their failure to serve themselves well, and it's easy to mistake that depth of feeling *about themselves* for the entirely different feeling of sorrow that is remorse for causing others harm. Emotional Predators might *appear* to have remorse, perhaps even saying something like they were "bad." But "bad" to them doesn't mean morally wrong (morals being a code responsive to the needs of others and a social community). To an Emotional Predator, "bad" means *not effective for themselves*. And the only effects they seek are ones that benefit them and assert their dominance.

Emotional Predators are expert at playing on the goodness, inexperience, busyness, and fears of decent people. For better or worse, most people don't want to see evil in their midst, or if they do see it, they "don't want to get involved," especially when the evil is cloaked in righteousness and victim-hood or operating from power. An Emotional Predator will spend mere moments throwing out a gripping story of his innocence and victim-hood (and of your badness), knowing it can take a lot of time and effort to pierce that facade. It's understandable that most people are too busy or tired or pre-occupied to look very far beneath the surface appearance of things. Most folks don't even bother with news media fact checking. Demagogue politicians count on this.

Our tendency to see and believe only the evidence that supports the beliefs we already hold (called confirmation bias) also inhibits our ability to look beyond our pre-conceived notions. Most people don't believe Emotional Predators are as bad as they are. Emotional Predators know this and use it when they lie to create a convincing, but false, positive image of themselves (and a negative image of their targets). They know most people won't see or believe even well-documented facts exposing them if those facts conflict with pre-existing beliefs about things like the inherent goodness of other people.

Emotional Predators are notorious for being *beguiling and seductive*, particularly with their new acquaintances. This makes dating a favorite playground for Emotional Predators (along with the courts) where they use their skill at presenting an emotionally compelling, but false, facade to great advantage. When getting to know a new person, an Emotional Predator immediately tunes into what the other person wants to see, and then she presents that persona. She also disarms the target's defense and alarm systems by feeding the target an image of a person the target feels safe with. Internet dating is particularly inviting to Emotional Predators because, without in-person contact to provide non-verbal clues, it's child's play for them to present online the words and "virtual" images of whatever the other person wants to see.

On a date or online, a decent person getting to know someone else thinks he's sharing personal things to develop intimacy. But an Emotional Predator is mining him for information about what's most important to him that she can use to manipulate him later. *An Emotional Predator will quickly know more about your core values and what is dearest to your heart than you do.* An Emotional Predator's use of information about you to manipulate and disarm you is why, as we'll see in Chapter 4, knowing core things about yourself is an essential part of a strong defense.

Emotional Predators are the consummate *charmers and entertainers* of our world. They are *bewitching chameleons* who change their facade to seduce and mislead as needed, presenting whatever image they think will most effectively get them what they want. Particularly with new acquaintances, Emotional Predators will appear charming, seductive, fun and sincere. They charm you at the beginning to get you involved with them, and they keep charming outsiders to prevent anyone from helping you stop their abuse. They play a game of "bait and switch," first making it all about you and what you want, need and value - *until* you take the bait and get hooked. Then they switch to their real agenda and make everything all about them. A woman described her last boyfriend as "super generous, considerate and gentle" when he was courting her. But soon after she let him move into her home, he became morose, started yelling and demanded she run his errands and clean up after him regardless of her work schedule. *In my experience, if someone you meet seems too good to be true, they probably are.*

When you're getting to know an Emotional Predator, he'll agree with you a lot. He'll pretend to share interests and experiences, giving you the false feeling that you have "so much" in common and that he's "just like" you. If you care about water quality, it'll be one of his concerns. If you're into salsa dancing, he'll have always wanted to take up dancing, but never met the right partner until you. If you need to take care of vulnerable people, he'll be concerned about the needy (or present *himself* as vulnerable). If you're a sucker for a doe eyed "innocent," he'll make himself appear as innocent as a new born babe. If you're not moved by innocence, but are impressed by strong-willed savvy confidence, that's the image of himself he'll sell you. In fact, he's nothing like you or the person you want or the persona he's selling. If your radar for Emotional Predators' deceptions isn't finely tuned, you won't find out soon enough.

Once you're involved with them, Emotional Predators will charm acquaintances and strangers as a way of *isolating you and cutting you off* from independent fact checking. An Emotional Predator will lower a "cone of silence" (apologies to Mel Brooks) around you without your permission and for no legitimate reason. After he's lured you in and you've taken the bait and you're committed to being involved with him, he'll begin to reveal his true selfish, abusive nature to you in private. *The more emotionally and financially dependent you are, the more free an Emotional Predator will feel to drop his charming seductive facade with you.* As he drops his facade, he'll shift his efforts to convincing you that the situation with him is normal and any discomfort you feel reflects something wrong with you. But he'll meticulously maintain his charming facade to everyone else. The parents at your children's events, school personnel, neighbors, work colleagues, and family may tell you how lucky you are to be with such a great guy, and they may think you're crazy if you suggest he's selfish, domineering, manipulative or abusive in the privacy of your home. This is part of gaslighting, which we'll look at in the next section of this chapter.

A kind and honest man allowed himself to be seduced into an affair with a "fantastic" married woman. She convinced him that she was the long suffering victim of her cold, bitter husband. She also insisted that, as her secret boyfriend, the kind man couldn't talk to anyone about his relationship with her, certainly not anyone who might know her husband and their situation. She discouraged the boyfriend from independent fact checking by warning him to protect her privacy within their circle of friends. She cleverly justified lowering this cone of silence around their relationship in part to protect her children from scandal. This meant the boyfriend couldn't independently verify her core stories of herself as her husband's victim. So the boyfriend's entire understanding of her situation with her husband was based only on what she told him. In fact, the cheating wife was an Emotional Predator victimizing both her husband and her boyfriend, and the boyfriend allowed himself to be cut off from independent information. In this situation, the boyfriend also repeatedly "opened his heart" to the wife, believing that he was creating intimacy, when he was just feeding her the information she needed to manipulate him.

Other Ways Emotional Predators Avoid Responsibility

As part of maintaining a false image, Emotional Predators avoid responsibility for the bad things they do. They do this in many ways. They'll *deny plain facts* and the reality that's obvious to anyone not already sucked into their universe. In the example from the start of Chapter 1, in violation of the court order, the Emotional Predator mother scheduled a nine day vacation with their daughter. When the father pointed this out, she flatly denied it, although it was a simple matter of counting days on a calendar. She even asserted indignantly that she "knew perfectly well how to read a calendar" - which might have been technically true, but was irrelevant to the fact that she'd intentionally scheduled more days than she was entitled to.

In fact, her admission that she knew how to read a calendar, while intended to throw the father on the defensive by implying that he'd unfairly accused her of not knowing how to read a calendar, served to prove that her scheduling too many days was intentional and not an accident. Bizarre as it may sound, *it's not uncommon for Emotional Predators to deny plain and incontrovertible facts, and express outrage that you dare confront them about it.*

Emotional Predators will *assert the opposite of reality* with absolute, unquestionable authority. And they can be very convincing, because they often believe their own distortions. Their universe really is all about them - they can't take anyone else's perspective, so they lack doubt. When she selfishly abuses and manipulates someone, an Emotional Predator will confidently congratulate herself for being "savvy" or "clever." The negative impact on the other person that would instill self-doubt in a decent person won't enter her mind, and this makes her sound so confident that her target can doubt his own experience of being abused. Decent people can be clever and savvy, resources that help protect them from Emotional Predators. But unlike Emotional Predators, decent people criticize themselves for any negative impact they have on another person - unless that person is an Emotional Predator and the negative impact is necessary for protection.

Sometimes Emotional Predators know full well they're lying through their teeth and they do this for profit, or just for the thrill of putting their audience off balance. *So an Emotional Predator's words can never be relied upon.* Remember, talk is cheap, particularly over the Internet. What people consistently *do* is more important than what they *say*. And, as we've seen, what they don't say can reveal more than what they do say.

When the facts aren't as objectively clear as counting days on a calendar, an Emotional Predator can throw a decent person off balance by *denying that events happened* the way their target saw or heard them happen. Without a recording to play back or some other independent documentation to verify how things actually occurred, the target is left confused and self-doubting. The more intensely and repeatedly an Emotional Predator protests his innocence, the more doubt a target or witness is likely to have. George Simon gives the example of a school bully who intentionally knocked another student's books to the ground in front of a hall monitor. The bully put on an innocent face and flatly denied he'd done anything. "I didn't do anything," he protested, implying *he* was the victim of the hall monitor's unfair accusation. Faced with the bully's vehement denial and implied counter-accusation, the hall monitor, being of good conscience and not wanting to falsely accuse a student, questioned whether she'd misinterpreted what she'd seen. Dr. Simon explains how this bully's intentional denial of plain fact is different from the unconscious psychological denial of things too emotionally upsetting to face, which is what traditional therapists mean when they talk about "being in denial."[10]

Emotional Predators also avoid responsibility by *playing the victim* and blaming others, particularly those they are victimizing. Emotional Predators will see their own disturbed behaviors and traits in others (this is called projection), which can make them sound convincing when they blame the person they're mistreating. Because Emotional Predators will project their own negative traits onto those around them, it's revealing to pay attention to the slurs and disparaging things someone says about others (and maybe about you). The negative things an Emotional Predator says about others can be an amazingly accurate description *of the Emotional Predator*. When someone repeatedly accuses you of things that were alien to you before you met that person, it's a clue that the accusations may be descriptions of the accuser who may be an Emotional Predator. If you've always been told you are generous and kind, and you now find yourself accused of being selfish and mean, you might've changed. But it's more likely that, through projection, your accuser is actually revealing that *they* are selfish and mean - and your accuser is probably an Emotional Predator.

I worked with an Emotional Predator who projected onto his ex-wife the anger he carried within him but refused to acknowledge, angrily attacking her while accusing *her* of being angry. His mother was an abusive, violent alcoholic through most of his childhood. He pretended to himself and others that he wasn't angry at his mother, claiming that growing up with her violent alcoholism didn't affect him at all as an adult. This Emotional Predator projected his own disowned anger at his mother onto his ex-wife, accusing her of being inherently angry while he maintained a soft spoken wide-eyed sad innocent facade. His facade took a seasoned psychologist to see through, but was convincing to police, teachers, and neighbors. The psychologist's evaluation aptly described him as angry, hostile, paranoid and depressed, beneath a sentimental, whimsical facade, and needing an absence of difference or disagreement in order to feel comfortable. The psychologist went on to describe other Emotional Predator traits in him, reporting that any disagreement with him was likely to be seen as hostile and observing that it was "almost as if you are either with him or against him."

But even professionals who see through an Emotional Predator's facade can have a hard time setting boundaries or calling out their inherent destructiveness. Perhaps understandably, most don't want to stick their necks out and be attacked or face the uphill battle of explaining a phenomenon that isn't widely understood in our society. In a failure typical of experts dealing with Emotional Predators, even though this psychologist reported the traits of a personality disorder in this father (which is a very serious mental illness), and found no evidence of a major mental health disorder in the mother (including no sign of the anger problem the father accused her of), the psychologist still recommended that their young children live with the Emotional Predator father half the time.

Emotional Predators see the world and other people as *either with them or against them*. They'll idealize you as "all good," which can be almost unimaginably seductive; who doesn't want to be seen as perfect by someone else? But without warning, they'll flip you from "all good" to "all bad." An Emotional Predator will seduce you with messages about how great you are (which sadly, often come as part of romance) only to attack you when they don't get everything they want from you at the moment they want it. After the romance has you hooked, they end the honeymoon, blaming you for almost anything. Flipping you from "all good" to "all bad" is a form of what psychoanalysis calls "splitting."

Briefly, splitting is what an immature mind does when it encounters negative and positive features in the same person (or situation). The immature mind can't tolerate these conflicting features in the same person, so it flips back and forth between all good and all bad. Splitting is a normal developmental stage for toddlers. A two year old will tell his mother that she's the greatest, and then a minute later when she tells him to wait for ice cream until after dinner, he'll scream that he hates her. Although normal for a two year old, that kind of splitting in an adult is a sign of serious problems. Mature responsible people can tolerate the ambiguity, ambivalence, frustrations and contradictions inherent in life.

In addition to avoiding conflicting features in the same person, flipping people to "all bad" also satisfies an Emotional Predator's need for enemies. Because all Emotional Predators are to some degree paranoid, *they must have enemies*. Having enemies is part of blaming others and not taking responsibility for their own behaviors and attitudes.

Emotional Predators can learn the rules of right and wrong and understand those ideas as intellectual abstractions about how to play a game, how to gain advantage over others and get what they want. Knowing the rules others follow teaches them how their targets' particular moral and ethical standards limit their target's ability to defend themselves. For example, the social rule "take turns" teaches the Emotional Predator to go in front of those who, as good citizens, are waiting for their turn. The social rule, "share your things," teaches an Emotional Predator to take what others share and give back only if he gains from it (or loses nothing). So pay attention to who tends to get things their way and who tends to give in, accommodate and acquiesce, and to whether someone applies rules only when it serves them.

Emotional Predators will ignore rules when it suits them, yet they'll insist others strictly follow rules when that suits them. An Emotional Predator mother whose son was seeing me for therapy didn't want the boy's father to know anything about the boy, so she reminded me repeatedly that his communications with me were confidential, even from his parents. Yet, when her son began asking *her* uncomfortable questions, she insisted on grilling me with questions about what he'd told me. When I reminded her that I wasn't able to share that information with her, she became nasty and threatening.

To weaken your ability to resist or think clearly, Emotional Predators will wear you down and exhaust you with endless stupid, irrational and often self-contradictory or hypocritical nonsense. They love to get you scurrying around on wild goose chases after irrelevant things. In addition to weakening your defenses, it gratifies their need to feel in control. I've seen many instances of an Emotional Predator accusing someone of saying something terrible in some unspecified prior email. To refute the accusation, the accused person has to spend hours going back through years of prior emails to confirm that they did *not* ever say what the Emotional Predator claims. Proving the negative - that you did *not* do or say something - can be nearly impossible.

But on the other hand, despite the lip service we give to "innocent until proven guilty," an uncontested accusation often is assumed to be true. (As we'll see in Chapter 7 about *Document and Keep Records*, this assumption that something not denied or corrected must be true can help you when you need to document something a teacher or other witness told you verbally.) Depending on the situation and the nature of the accusation, it may be best to simply deny an accusation, ask the Emotional Predator for proof, and resist the temptation to spend hours sifting through old emails and records to prove it false.

Another subtle assault Emotional Predator's favor is *confusing and disorienting you by disrupting your natural rhythms*. Calling you at work when she knows you're in meetings, keeping you up after you would normally have gone to bed, waking you in the middle of the night and peppering you with questions, demanding you do things on her schedule are some of the ways an Emotional Predator can disrupt your natural rhythms. The tactic of disrupting your rhythm is a very subtle and effective way to put you off balance in a way that's hard to notice. Are you constantly being rushed? Is a quick thing taking forever? Is a straightforward, simple matter being needlessly complicated? Is someone repeatedly disrupting your sleep? If so, you're probably dealing with an Emotional Predator.

Closely related to disrupting your natural rhythms, Emotional Predators will sometimes present a constantly moving target of shifting demands, requirements or "concerns." No matter what you do, he's never satisfied. As we've seen, when an Emotional Predator is consistently inconsistent, you find yourself in a frustrating game of whack-a-mole where you satisfy what he's demanded only to find a new, different demand pop up. This keeps you always blamed for being inadequate and failing and causing the problems (which is blaming the victim). And it diverts your attention from what's really going on.

Disrupting your rhythms and never being satisfied provokes visible frustration, confusion and anger in you, while the Emotional Predator's passive aggression remains hidden. It's useful to remember that you're not inadequate because someone else isn't satisfied and failure to plan on someone else's part doesn't constitute an emergency on your part. And through all of this, an Emotional Predator will isolate you to keep you from getting a reality check or validating your own instincts that something is wrong with the way she's treating you.

Being targeted by an Emotional Predator can be especially traumatic because the she'll induct you into her distorted world, and separate you from anyone who would keep you in touch with your wider more self-protecting reality. Like a frog who won't jump out of a pot if the water is brought to a boil slowly, you find you don't notice you've been slowly cut off from friends and family who could offer you a reality-based, healthy perspective. As you become more involved with the Emotional Predator, she'll pick fights or be negative when she interacts with your friends. Then if you try to see your friends without her, she'll punish you, by picking a fight or giving you the cold freeze as you get ready to go out or after you return.

Isolating a target is part of the tactic of *gaslighting*. Gaslighting is a form of mental abuse in which a victim is manipulated into doubting their own memory, perception and sanity by an abuser who does things like denying that previous abusive incidents ever occurred and staging bizarre events in order to disorient the victim. Watching the 1944 film *Gaslight* is a great way to understand what gaslighting is like. Gaslighting cannot work if the target remains in close and frequent contact with good, trustworthy people who'll contradict the distorted reality the Emotional Predator is trying to impose. Being with an Emotional Predator is like living with fun-house mirrors that distort your reflection. It's vital to get out to others who have non-distorting mirrors that the Emotional Predator has no contact with, and take a good long look at yourself and your situation in those accurate mirrors.

Psychologically, gaslighting can be seen as form of *projective identification*, a concept not well understood, where the disturbed Emotional Predator makes the target feel crazy. I'll explain Projective Identification in detail in Chapter 6. Briefly, it's a way Emotional Predators avoid responsibility by manipulating your emotions to *provoke in you the inner turmoil that they can't handle* and push out of their own awareness. They do this most often through passive aggression, withholding things you're well within your rights to expect and receive. Once you take the bait and react in frustration, they focus attention on your *reaction*, blaming you for your very human response to the hurtfulness of what they're *not* doing. Of course, what they're *not* doing - what they're withholding - is invisible to most people, while what you do or say in frustrated reaction is easy to see.

A common example of passive aggression is the spouse who withholds sex and affection as a punishment or weapon.[11] An Emotional Predator might starve her husband for sex and affection, then blame him when he seeks it elsewhere. But an Emotional Predator's passive aggressive withholding can be as simple as repeatedly not showing up on time, or not answering the phone or texts at times when the caller/texter obviously needs some logistical information. This is common when divorced Emotional Predators impede the smooth drop off or pick up of children by the other parent. Not letting yourself be provoked stymies an Emotional Predator's effort to avoid responsibility by blaming you for what they provoke through projective identification. As we'll see in Chapter 6, being unprovoked is essential to a strong defense.

How They Use Words to Mislead

Emotional Predators often can be spotted by their pliable approach to words. Most words carry many shades of meaning, and the specific meaning of any particular word choice is determined mostly by context - by the surrounding facts and situation - and by tone and expression, which are mostly missing from writings. To distort reality, Emotional Predators will ignore the relevant context, over simplify, state untrue or incomplete facts, and use innuendo. They'll ignore plain meanings; shift between vagueness and precision; use passive voice, pop-psych jargon, and absolutes.

Emotional Predators will subtly *twist or ignore the plain meaning of words* that you or they use. For example, you might pay for a teenager's parking ticket even though you have strong reservations about enabling the teenager, but an Emotional Predator will twist this to imply that, *because* you paid it, you *wanted* to pay for it. In fact, our motivations can be complicated and conflicted. Sometimes we do things we don't *want* to do but we know are necessary or the best alternative, like changing a baby's diaper. But an Emotional Predator will twist the shades of meaning of words to *imply* motives and feelings that aren't actually there, either in you or her. This is a subtle way of reversing the truth.

Emotional Predators can *shift between vague and precise language* as it suits their needs. This is similar to an Emotional Predator breaking rules when it suits her and insisting that others follow rules when that suits her. She'll use vague language to suggest or imply something without actually saying it. Then when you try to hold her to what any normal person would understand her words to mean, she'll resort to a narrow technical legalistic interpretation of what she did - and did not - say. This is stock in trade for some lawyers.

The topic between two divorced parents was summer camps that included a tennis camp. On one part of its website the tennis club called the tennis camp a "training." The father had stated in email "I will pay for their camps," but when it came time to pay for the tennis camp, this Emotional Predator refused to pay, claiming it was a "training" and that he'd only agreed to pay for "camps." This kind of legalistic wriggling out of responsibilities is standard Emotional Predator behavior. So it pays to be clear with your words, and to monitor closely how another person uses his, and particularly how his words do or do not match his deeds. If you're not particularly good at word games, a savvy lawyer can help parse things and state things clearly (or vaguely) as needed. Being strategically vague or clear as needed with an Emotional Predator is a way of playing his word games better than he plays them.

Using *passive voice* is one way to be vague. Passive voice is a particular way of constructing a sentence so that the subject of the sentence is acted on by the verb (instead of acting on the verb). For example, in "The ball was thrown," the ball (the subject of the sentence) receives the action of the verb, and "was thrown" is in the passive voice, leaving it unknown *who* did the throwing. An active voice construction would be "The pitcher threw the ball," which identifies the actor (the true subject). An Emotional Predator will speak in passive voice as a way of being vague and avoiding responsibility. An Emotional Predator will say "the barn didn't get painted," rather than "I didn't paint the barn." There are legitimate stylistic and other reasons for using passive voice, but it's useful to notice when someone is using it to be evasive, what they're evading and why.

Emotional Predators love to *use pop-psychology, new age and politically correct language* to evade and manipulate. This is a way of playing on popular, but not well founded, cultural biases and norms. Consider this example of a skillful Emotional Predator using vague and empty but politically correct words to *look* sincere, conciliatory and apologetic, while continuing to ignore the facts and avoid acknowledging his bad behaviors. A father had promised his sixteen year old daughter equipment she needed for school. When the daughter asked for it, the father insisted that the daughter first meet with him, saying he needed to explain how unfair things were to him. Sounds like a reasonable request for open communication between father and daughter. But look at the context. He was failing to

STEP 1 - IDENTIFY THEM | 73

keep his commitment and promise. He was holding the equipment *hostage* to extort what he wanted, and one thing he wanted was to be seen as the victim. Another thing he wanted was to assert his domination and power by forcing the daughter to meet with him. When the daughter held her ground, refusing to meet the father *until he first kept his prior promise*, he ramped up his effort to manipulate with an email full of pop-psych, new age, politically correct jargon.

> "I know you're mad at me and do believe you have reason to be angry. I know I've let you down over the years and want to apologize for that. I'm ready and willing to hear what you have to say to me. Mis-communication and conflict happen in all close relationships. If you meet with me, I'm sure we can get to a better place. The next step is to acknowledge and hear what's going on for each of us and try to get to a place of mutual understanding. I respect you so much. I'm sure we can get to a better place."

This email is typical of the kind of empty, pop-psych jargon Emotional Predators use. Let's look at it section by section. My comments are inserted in parenthesis after each quoted section. "I know you're mad at me and do believe you have reason to be angry. I know I've let you down over the years and want to apologize for that." ("Let you down," without specifying exactly how, is meaningless. "Over the years" also is vague. The father does not mention his recent *specific* bad act: his refusal to keep his promise to deliver the equipment that occurred within the month.) "I'm ready and willing to hear what you have to say to me." (The *daughter* had nothing to say to the father, it was the *father's* agenda to force his daughter to listen to his sad "victim" story.) "Mis-communication and conflict happen in all close relationships." (This general statement in *passive voice* sounds true enough, but leaves out the subject of the sentence, the *actor* who caused the problem: the father. The father uses passive voice here to evade taking responsibility for his specific bad act. The conflict was caused by the father and the only "mis-communication" was his failure to deliver what he had promised.) "If you meet with me, I'm sure we can get to a better place." (The Emotional Predator always thinks that complying with *his* agenda will make things better.) "The next step is to acknowledge and hear what's going on for each of us and try to get to a place of mutual understanding. I respect you so much. I'm sure we can get to a better place." (This means that the only way the Emotional Predator will get to a better place is if he gets the dominance meeting he wants. If he truly respected her, he would've delivered what he'd promised instead of holding it hostage. The next step for a decent person would be to deliver the school equipment he'd promised.)

Go back and read the entire email again. Do you see that the Emotional Predator offers no capitulation or acknowledgment that he's holding hostage something he'd promised to deliver? Can you see through the vague jargon to the father's effort to get the daughter to capitulate to the father's agenda - to dominate and plead victimhood? The father was insisting on a meeting *before* he'd keep his promise. He sent lots of politically correct words to cover over his real agenda: avoid acknowledging his bad act, exert dominance by forcing a meeting in which he could play the victim, extort what he wanted by holding hostage what the daughter needed and manipulate the daughter through guilt. And of course, the entire situation of withholding something he'd promised is textbook passive-aggression.

Another clue to spotting an Emotional Predator is the way they tend to use *absolute language*. Pay attention when someone uses words like always/never, all/nothing, good/bad, right/wrong, etc. These kinds of words leave out the larger context of situation and probabilities - the shades of grey, ambiguity and ambivalence inherent in human affairs. And these absolute words are moralizing and emotionally manipulative, designed to evoke guilt in people who have a well developed conscience. Words like legitimate/illegitimate, appropriate/inappropriate, reasonable/unreasonable are other more subtle, politically correct ways of pushing people into a false black or white, all or nothing morality trap.

An Emotional Predator will use absolute words to pressure you into being on the "correct" side of things, and to induce guilt by suggesting you're on the "wrong" side of things. Of course, the "correct" side of things is whatever side serves the Emotional Predator and the "wrong" side of things is the side that doesn't serve him. Trying to please him or blaming yourself for not satisfying him plays right into his hands. But your life isn't a melodramatic morality play soap opera in which you have to strive to meet an abusive person's absolute standards for you - unless you choose to write that story for yourself.

In summary, Emotional Predators do many things to dominate and avoid taking responsibility. Their tactics overlap and they use many of them together, all designed to manipulate your emotions to get you to submit and take responsibility for their shortcomings. An Emotional Predator will *pretend to be innocent*. She will *pretend to be oblivious and ignorant*. Don't be fooled. She knows what she's doing. An Emotional Predator will *offer excuses and justifications* (and blame others), rather than change to accommodate someone else's legitimate needs, particularly if she would be inconvenienced by accommodating the other person. An Emotional Predator will *project her own inner disturbance* onto others, seeing her own troubles in them, and use *projective identification* to provoke in her targets the uncomfortable feelings she herself can't handle. She'll *apply rules only when it serves her.* She'll *dodge direct questions* and *twist the plain meaning* of words. She'll *flip you* from "all good" to "all bad," attacking you when she used to worship you. She'll *wear you down* with irrelevant or hypocritical nonsense. And she'll *disrupt your natural rhythms* to put you off balance and *divert your attention* from what she's up to.

As we've seen, when we look at the tactics of Emotional Predators, it's important to remember that decent people also can use them on occasion, either for defense or as a temporary stress reaction. In fact, using those tactics selectively - taking a page from an Emotional Predator's play book - is often the most effective way to defend yourself and your loved ones. But Emotional Predators use those tactics repeatedly and indiscriminately, and that (along with other things) distinguishes them from decent people.

COMMON ATTITUDES AND PROFESSIONS

In addition to the behaviors and tactics that distinguish Emotional Predators, recognizing their *attitudes about themselves and others* and being aware of *the professions they are attracted to*, also helps you spot them. Attitudes are inner states that reflect in behaviors that you can observe, mostly with your eyes and ears. But picking up on attitudes also can involve *tuning into your intuition or sixth sense* a bit more. Listening to your gut feelings, paying attention to when the hair on the back of your neck stands up or when you have a queasy feeling in the pit of your stomach can help you notice the troublesome attitudes common among Emotional Predators. Tuning into an Emotional Predator's attitudes can be like hearing the music rather than listening to the individual notes of a song. Picking up on his attitude can happen quickly, even instantly, or it may take longer to gather the data about his behaviors to confirm your gut suspicion. In Chapter 4 about *Ways to Know Yourself Better*, we'll take a close look at Carl Jung's ideas about the different ways we know what we know.

Emotional Predators can be *arrogant and entitled*, particularly when their tactics bring them financial, social or political success. They can be self-aggrandizing braggarts, taking every opportunity to let you know how wonderful they are and how lucky you are to be around them. They can be self-righteous, as though the nasty and manipulative things they do are "of course" justified and reasonable, and there's something wrong with you for questioning or doubt-ing them. They can be condescending. Or, on the other hand, they can pretend to be meek, humble and self-effacing. Either extreme is suspicious.

Because Emotional Predators believe they're better than every-one else and that the world owes them whatever they want, when they don't get their way, they can become *impatient, intolerant or ir-ritated* - or worse. To really know someone, you must observe them when they're faced with genuine adversity. How do they act when things aren't going their way or when they're forced to delay gratify-ing their desires? For an Emotional Predator, the universe and all the people in it exist to serve them and it violates the proper order of things if they aren't getting what they want. When she's not get-ting what she wants, or if you criticize her, an Emotional Predator is likely to be unpleasant in a number of ways - impatient, intolerant, irritated, dismissive, angry or aggressive - or she may play for your sympathy by pretending to be a bewildered, innocent martyr.

Another attitude common to Emotional Predators is *cockiness and a lack of humility*. The self-confidence of an Emotional Predator tends to express in displays of excessive sincerity, focus or self-assurance. Although it's hard to fault someone for seeming sincere, focused or confident and self-assured, an Emotional Predator's displays of self-confidence also include elements of contempt for others, disdain for authority, bravado and heroics. True heroes do not display heroics.

Emotional Predators are drawn to professions where they can exercise power over others - particularly jobs where they can hide under the cover of respected authority. Some of their favorite professions include politics, law (lawyers, judges and law enforcement), education, spiritual leadership (priests, imams, rabbis, gurus and spiritual guides), medicine, corporate management, sales, civil service, and mental health. The common quality of these professions is they provide access to people who are emotionally vulnerable and powerless relative to the professional.

Of course being in one of those professions doesn't mean someone is an Emotional Predator, and these professions also attract wonderful decent people who sincerely want to help vulnerable people. And of course, Emotional Predators aren't only in these professions. They can lurk anywhere, in every institution and community. But professions that offer power over others attract Emotional Predators, so those professions tend to have a higher percentage of Emotional Predators in them.

Being in a profession of power isn't proof someone is an Emotional Predator. It's just an additional warning sign to notice along with other things. If you look at people you know in these professions in light of the behaviors, attitudes and traits of Emotional Predators, you may see some of them in a different light. So it's smart to be alert when dealing with anyone whose job offers power over vulnerable people.

The legal and penal systems involve particularly vulnerable and powerless people. Lawyers learn a special language that the rest of us can't understand, which gives a lawyer special power to translate information we need from legalese into common language. Family courts control people's children, which for most parents is the most emotionally vulnerable part of their lives. Parents in the family court system can be subjected to inspection of the most minute personal details of their life. Married couples are rarely subjected to that kind of privacy invasion and judgment, even though married parents can be tremendously dysfunctional.

An often invisible part of the legal system is the administrative and licensing boards that wield power over regulated people and licensees' ability to earn a living. Like many similar jobs, abuse in these forums can hide behind platitudes about protecting the public. An attorney with thirty five years' experience dealing with a medical licensing board told me that, although the board sometimes protected the public, most of its efforts went to mindlessly bullying good doctors over trivia. He thought that inept professionals who enjoy lording it over their more competent colleagues are drawn to work on licensing boards the way neighbors who enjoy controlling other people's homes are drawn to serve on home owner's association boards.

Emotional Predators are highly motivated to climb the corporate ladder to positions where they have power over subordinates and earn lots of money that they can use to control others. They'll climb toward the top (or wherever else they want to be) without a care for who they step on to get there, enjoying the stepping. In Chapter 2, I mentioned the example of "Chainsaw Dunlop," a CEO who was brought in to fire employees for the short term profit of corporate buyout speculators. Dunlop readily admitted in interviews that he had the traits of a psychopath: ruthlessness, lack of concern for the negative impact on others of his actions, selfishness, etc... Jim Edwards, the founding editor of Business Insider has written that psychopaths are found in greater proportions among CEOs. He cites the estimate of a study by Bond University psychologist Nathan Brooks that "between 3% and 21% of CEOs are probably psychopaths," compared with around one percent of the normal population.[12] (Remember, psychopaths are only one variety of Emotional Predator.)

Emotional Predators are good at climbing organizational ladders. So if you encounter one of them at a middle level of an organization, seeking help higher up in the hierarchy can be perilous, because you may be appealing for help to a more accomplished Emotional Predator. And *sometimes Emotional Predators enjoy ganging up together* to dominate. Adolph Hitler and Joseph Goebbels are a good example of this.

At the time of this writing, allegations about powerful men's (and a few women's) sexual abuse of people (mostly women) have broken into common awareness. On both sides of the political spectrum, from conservative Fox news personalities like Bill O'Reilly to the liberal movie producer, Harvey Weinstein, the public is becoming aware of men who (allegedly) used their power over the careers of actresses, actors and employees to sexually abuse them, and the power of their wealth to use lawyers and payments to silence them afterwards. A few initial accusations have triggered an outpouring of similar accusations against many men in a variety of positions of power.[13] In these situations, it's the position or exercise of *power* that makes the act abusive, rather than just a clumsy come on or a consensual encounter someone later regrets.

In each era, "experts" with special access to the current state-of-the-art "truth" - the sacred wisdom of the day - wield power over the rest of the population. Today we laugh at many of yesterday's "state of the art" theories, treatments and approaches. One need look no farther than the abandoned medical practices of applying leeches, giving infants and children morphine to quiet them, or using mercury as a cure, or lobotomies as a treatment for anxiety or depression, or amphetamines for weight loss, or drilling holes in the skull (trepanation) to cure migraines. A doctor doing those things back when they were considered state of the art medicine would've had respect and power. A doctor doing those things today would have no respect or power. She'd probably be barred from practicing medicine.

In the near future, many of today's state of the art theories, treatments and approaches will be laughed at. *But the role of expertise in creating power over others remains relatively constant throughout the ages.* The placebo effect of a person's *belief* that someone or something can help them is very powerful, particularly in medicine. And people seeking expert care in medicine and elsewhere can be particularly needy and scared. Although it's out of fashion these days, some doctors (and experts in other fields) still indulge in subtle *"expertise" dominance*, asserting as unassailable truth things that are really just the current state of knowledge and belief, things that'll be replaced and maybe even laughed at in a few decades.

Perhaps most ironic, the mental health field attracts a particularly devious type of Emotional Predator who hides his power tripping behind the cloak of expertise and "helping." There are few better places to exercise government sanctioned power over a constant supply of emotionally vulnerable people than the mental health professions. "A diagnosis of mental illness can remove your children from you, oblige you to undergo treatments against your will"[14] and deprive you of your liberty. And mental health diagnoses are far from scientifically based, reflecting more the trends and biases of the moment. More than you may be comfortable accepting, mental health workers use psychological and emotional jargon, and the leverage of expertise, to manipulate. Nurse Ratchet in Ken Kesey's *One Flew Over the Cuckoo's Nest* is a particularly brazen and sadistic fictional example of an Emotional Predator in a mental health field. The movie starring Jack Nicholson is instructive.

An elementary school counselor needed permission from parents before talking with a third grader. Because of the counselor's previous dishonesty, the student's parents instructed the principal and counselor that the counselor wasn't permitted to speak with their child. Ignoring the rules when it suited her, this counselor waited until the student was alone in a room, leaned over the child and said to her, "I know I'm not supposed to talk to you, but I'm wondering who told you not to talk to me?" The child, being smarter than the counselor and not intimidated, stared up at the counselor and said nothing. The counselor repeated "I know I'm not supposed to talk to you, but I'm wondering who told you not to talk to me?" Same response from the child. The counselor tried the same thing a third time, met the same silence and gave up. It's a rare child who can stand up to that kind of adult authority figure intimidation and misconduct. It's typical of Emotional Predators to ignore rules and try to intimidate a less powerful person, in this case from the role of counselor "helper."

Likewise, teachers and education administrators control the daily environment of children, a particularly powerless group that needs approval and sanction (i.e. grades) from the teacher. I've noticed two types of people seem drawn to education: those who delight in the opening of young minds and those who glory in lording over powerless young people. The Emotional Predator disguised as classroom teacher or school administrator may be a largely overlooked hidden bullying problem. That could account for the large number of bright children who quietly regard teachers with contempt and school as a demeaning hoop to jump through.

Religious leaders, who wield the ultimate power of threatening eternal damnation in an afterlife, and politicians, who wield the real power of changing society's rules (and of directing where money flows) are two obvious professions that attract Emotional Predators. Politicians on both sides of the political spectrum can be Emotional Predators, but illustrating the maxim that we tend to see what we want to see, people on the right tend to see those traits only in politicians on the left and people on the left tend to see them only in politicians on the right. Similarly, religious folks can see abominable traits in religious leaders of *other* religions, but find it hard to see them in their own religious leaders.

TECHNIQUES AND TIPS FOR SPOTTING EMOTIONAL PREDATORS

To distinguish decent people from the seductive and disarming facades presented by Emotional Predators, you need to become a close observer and a smart tester. To be a more accurate observer, cultivate the scientist's *impartial observing stance*, which is very similar to the Buddhist stance of *non-attached witnessing*. These states of mind are detached from any desired outcome, with as few pre-conceived expectations as possible, open to whatever presents itself. In these states, the filters created by our unexamined stories are less active and we're not pushing out of our awareness certain information while highlighting others. When we unconsciously filter, we experience another person as a significant person from our childhood, not as the person he really is. But in a scientific or Buddhist witnessing stance our vision is less filtered, thus clearer.

Our stories about ourselves and others, and the emotions they elicit in us, interfere with our ability to see things as they are. When we're emotionally invested or emotionally triggered, we don't see clearly. When we're calm and emotionally neutral, we see better. As Anias Nin famously put it, "We don't see things the way they are. We see things the way we are." The Rock Man from the movie *The Point* perhaps less famously put it, "You see what you want to see and you hear what you want to hear."[15]

The impact of the self-fulfilling prophesies embedded in our stories shouldn't be underestimated. *We tend to get what we expect.* The well-documented placebo effect is a manifestation of this. So when trying to identify an Emotional Predator, it's important to *recognize the things you expect or want to see.* For example, if you want to see good in everyone and hate that untrustworthy people force you to change your trusting stance, then you won't *want* to see the Emotional Predator right before your eyes (Emotional Predators are always untrustworthy). Good, decent people are a mixture of positive and negative features. Looking for only good in others is a trap for being deceived by an Emotional Predator who'll sell you the "all good" persona that you want to see.

Someone who appears to be "too good to be true" probably is. As part of her seduction, an Emotional Predator at first will appear to be an ideal you've dreamed of. So look for rough edges and imperfections in other people. Ask yourself whether you're making excuses for another person. Although you may want harmony and agreement with others, pay attention when another person disagrees with you. Disagreeing respectfully can be a sign of decency. In all of this, *observe yourself and others without agenda, expectation or desire to see any particular thing* good or bad, without judging or moralizing or being self-righteous.

As a general matter, it's important not to share your investigative process and skeptical thoughts with the person you're investigating (unless the person you're investigating is you). Strange as it may sound, you can't count on getting reliable information about a person by asking *him* to verify something about himself. *Your questions usually tell more about you than the person being questioned.* Because we tend to ask about what we care about, when you ask an Emotional Predator a question, you're probably revealing what's important to you. Asking an Emotional Predator "are you honest?" or "do you think relationships should be based on trust?" simply alerts an Emotional Predator to the importance *to you* of honesty and trust, and instructs him to manipulate you by presenting a facade of honesty and trustworthiness.

When a woman started to wonder if her new boyfriend was withdrawing to punish her, she asked him "did you stop texting back because you were withdrawing and punishing me, or did you have to start a work meeting?" This Emotional Predator welcomed the ready-made excuse she'd provided and assured her that he'd just had to start a work meeting and that he'd never withdraw or punish her. From her question, he learned that she valued staying engaged and not with-drawing in relationships. He also learned that she was vulnerable to feeling punished by being abandoned. He used this knowledge to manipulate her by punishing her with frequent abandonments and, if she questioned him, inducing guilt by pretending to be hurt that she would suspect him of bad motives. Claiming to be the victim of the person they're victimizing is standard Emotional Predator practice. Only by *paying attention to his behaviors over time instead of asking him about his intentions*, was she able to notice that whenever she didn't do what he wanted, he withdrew and punished her.

There are many things you can do to sharpen your powers of observation and test the data your observations produce. One of them is to *look for consistent patterns over a broad range of instances and circumstances.* You're looking for an overall constellation not one or two instances. As we've seen, some of the behaviors or traits of Emotional Predators can show up in decent people from time to time for a number of reasons. It's well said that, under stress, even good people regress to more primitive ways of being. And remember that you aren't an Emotional Predator if you strategically probe and test someone with techniques that are clever, but not fully truthful.

In observing someone, it's useful to *tune into subtle energy flows* between you and them. Notice whether, over time, the encounters consistently drain you while they energize the other person. Who does the heavy lifting to keep the relationship going? Is the flow of effort a one-way street? When you feel drained, does the other person seem light and enlivened? What happens when you ask for a break or for the other person to pick up some slack or take some of the load?

As we've seen, it's useful to look at someone's words and what their words mean in a dictionary, and to consider what their words do *not* mean. Make direct, simple requests, and only accept direct, clear answers. Is the person you are talking to being vague? Have they given you a lot of talk, but still left your question unanswered?

But perhaps more importantly, without being asked or reminded, do they follow up with actions to implement their stated intentions? Like a stereotypical bad parent who says "Do as I say, not as I do," an Emotional Predator will want you to focus on what he says, not on what he does. Although you can learn a lot from what Emotional Predators do and don't say, you usually learn more from the actions they do and don't take, and comparing their words with their actions and omissions.

Talk is cheap. Actions speak louder than words. Statements of intention and plans can be important, but have little value by themselves. There's no substitute for looking carefully at what someone actually does, particularly in relation to what they say. So when they're not congruent, relay on what people *do*, rather than what they *say*.

But sometimes paying close attention to what someone says by itself provides enough information. A client of mine texting with a woman he was thinking of dating saw enough from those texts to know he needed to steer clear of her. This women wrote him "you pick the restaurant" for their second date. That's all she said. When he picked a pub, she wrote back "well, if you really want burgers and beer, then how about ..." and named another pub. On its face, this looks pretty innocent. But look more closely. She told him to *pick*. She didn't tell him to *suggest*. When he did as she directed, she made an implied accusation that "burgers and beer" were inferior ("well, if you *really* want ...") and suggested another place that was virtually the same. This exposed her need to have things "her way": going to the same kind of place, but one that was *her* pick. It also showed her need to control the communications, and that she'd set up a "no-win" bind for him: he had to pick, but when he did, she complained. She also subtly tried to put him on the defensive by implying that his choice was sub-par. And she mis-characterized the place he picked and what he "wanted" (in fact, his pick offered much more than just burgers and beer, and he liked neither burgers nor beer). She was too lazy to spend two minutes googling the menu of the place he picked to see that it offered much more than burgers and beer, inviting him to do all the research and then justify and explain his pick to her - again from a position of *defending* his pick to her.

Does it seem like I'm reading too much into a short text? When he tested his impression that she was a dangerous person by politely pointing out to her that she'd told him to pick, that she'd made a number of inaccurate assumptions and that her pick was virtually the same as his, she clearly exposed her true Emotional Predator nature, sending him a series of long incoherent nasty rambling accusing texts. He, sensibly, deleted her texts and blocked her number. He chose to share with her the three things he'd observed about her communication only to test his initial impression that she was dangerous. As we'll see in Chapter 7, if he'd been involved with her instead of just deciding whether to have a second date, he'd have been better served by *knowing* what he observed without showing it to her.

Testing Out What You Observe

Testing what you've observed can be an crucial part of distinguishing decent people from Emotional Predators. One way to test someone's words is to *see if they'll "put their money where their mouth is" and follow through* with congruent actions, particularly when those actions cost or inconvenience them. A related way to test the sincerity of someone's assurances is to ask them to put them in writing. When you do this, an Emotional Predator will often reply indignantly and accuse you of having something wrong with you because you don't trust them enough to just take their word. That's a strategy of blaming the victim to put the victim on the defensive. When someone objects to writing down their promises, I'm fairly sure they aren't trustworthy.

One way to test for whether someone is dodging responsibility is to see if he *avoids giving a direct answer to a simple question or request.* Notice if he avoids answering or strays off topic when the topic is his bad behaviors or something he doesn't want to address. A client's ex-husband owed her $5,000. For over a decade in which he earned a very comfortable income and put many tens of thousands of dollars into his savings account, whenever she asked him to pay what he owed her, he simply replied "I'm not interested in talking about the past." *"Not interested"* because there was only loss and no gain for him. In textbook Emotional Predator fashion, ten years later when he wanted her to agree to take on $15,000 of an extravagant $30,000 annual expense for their children - an expense that he'd just incurred without consulting her, he suddenly acknowledged his ten year old $5,000 debt and told her she could deduct that from the new $15,000 payment he wanted her to take on. *He acknowledged his debt and offered to pay it only when doing so served him.* Getting $10,000 from her that year ($15,000 minus the $5,000), and $15,000 in the next few years was worth finally paying his $5,000 debt that he hadn't been "interested in" for years.

Another way to distinguish Emotional Predators is to test for actions and responses. Try setting a boundary and see whether it's consistently respected, or ignored and disrespected. You might tell someone you can't take calls or texts when you're at work, and see if they find reasons why they "have to" call or text you then. You might try denying someone's request to spend time with you and see if they try to convince you to relent. You're looking to see if they accept and honor your boundary without pressuring you to change it. A decent person will respect your boundaries and support you in maintaining them, even if your boundaries aren't pleasant for them. If she doesn't like your boundary, an Emotional Predator will try to change your mind with guilt, blaming, bullying, hostility, bribery, threats to abandon or anything else that would leverage your emotions.

Emotional Predators are chameleons, changing colors to fit in with whatever you show them you want or value. One way to test this is to pretend to have an interest or value, and see if the other person switches to sharing that interest or value. If another person presents themselves as liking something you like, try later saying you like something else instead and see if they shift to presenting themselves as liking the new thing. A decent person might be willing to try something you're interested in, but they won't pretend it's their own interest. Emotional Predators will try to convince you that they're "just like" you and the two of you have "so much" in common. They present a shifting facade that morphs into whatever you say you desire. That's different from a multi-faceted person who's open to trying a wide range of new interests and things.

So be cautious with people who appear to offer you something you might want. For years, part of my practice and interest has been conflict mitigation and mediation. I was approached by an Emotional Predator from two states away masquerading as a "conflict-ending" academic and professional. This fellow offered to hire me as a mediation "trainer" to train mediators around the country. He cleverly set up our communications as an "interview" to see if I would make the grade to be "hired" by him. He tried to make me feel like I needed to please him: holding up a carrot for me to chase. When I mentioned a book project I was working on, this Emotional Predator perked up with "we can publish that." But when I asked direct questions about when his trainings were actually scheduled, how many students were signed up and how exactly he could publish my manuscript, he was evasive and didn't answer. Instead, he said a lot of vague things about conflict resolution generally. It quickly became clear that no trainings were scheduled or existed, and he had no ability to publish.

For a while I was perplexed about what he was really up to, so I played along and feigned interest, all the time testing and watching carefully. He was slick. To see though his facade, I had to use Emotional Predator tactics, like pretending to be interested in his "job" when I wasn't, and concealing my true doubts about him while pretending to be enthusiastic and compliant. One test was to separately ask the same questions of his training coordinator and him. When their answers conflicted and the coordinator abruptly moved to a different job on the other side of the country and wouldn't answer my emails about the job she'd just left, it strongly suggested something wasn't right.

To test this Emotional Predator and discover his real intentions, I pretended to be eager to please him and do what he wanted, letting out rope for him to hang himself with. He finally sent me an outrageously overreaching "non-compete" agreement that was worded to prevent me from providing in my local area the mediation services I'd been providing there for decades. By stringing him along, I finally saw what his real game was. His real aim was to enter my state's mediation market after first eliminating the existing local competition with onerous non-competition agreements - agreements for which he would deliver nothing but empty promises about nonexistent trainer jobs and publishing capacity. In short, he'd made up an elaborate ruse of empty promises in a scheme to eliminate competition from a market that he wanted to enter. This only became clear after I tested him by playing the Emotional Predator game of deception (telling him what he wanted to hear) better than he did. I walked away, without giving in to my Ego desire to tell him how I saw through him.

To see Emotional Predators clearly, it's helpful to maintain a healthy dose of skepticism. Being skeptical and discerning isn't the same as being paranoid or being immersed in negativity. You can take a hard look and do some testing, while remaining open to being pleasantly surprised. Part of being skeptical includes being a vigorous investigator and independent fact checker.

It's easy and natural to accept a new love interest's negative stories about her ex, without asking whether her ex might have a completely different story - one that might fill in important facts your love interest has left out as part of lying by omission to you. The lack of independent verification of another person's stories is a warning flag. Background checks are readily available online and you can gain a world of useful information talking with co-workers, ex-spouses and others who have long experience with the person you're investigating. Try to find out if a person has filed lawsuits, complaints or licensing grievances, often a favorite pastime of Emotional Predators. It can take time for an Emotional Predator to show her true colors, so observe over time and repeated experiences. Over time, she'll consistently violate the norms of decency in the ways we've been looking at.

But the most important resource for spotting Emotional Predators is your knowledge of *yourself*, particularly your emotional triggers and values. Your emotional reactions can be a blinder or a reliable guide, depending on how well you know yourself, particularly what triggers you and what you want and value. The more dispassionate you are about yourself, the more accurately you'll know yourself. The more accurately you know yourself, the more clearly and quickly you can see an Emotional Predator. A particularly important thing to notice about yourself is how your current inner states may differ from before you became involved with another person. Are you more confused, angry, ashamed, depressed, guilty or frustrated? Were you like that before this person entered your life? Be honest with yourself, *but not with a suspected Emotional Predator*, about yourself. Later in Chapter 7 as part of *controlling information*, we'll look more closely at the vital importance of not letting an Emotional Predator know what you know about yourself.

chapter four

Step 2 - How to Know Your Emotionally Vulnerable Places Better Than an Emotional Predator Does

Knowing yourself is the foundation of every strategy
for protecting yourself.

"You can try to run, but you can't hide from what's inside of you."
Walter Becker and Donald Fagen

*"There are three things extremely hard: steel, a diamond,
and to know one's self."*
Ben Franklin

KNOWING YOURSELF IS THE CORE OF ALL DEFENSES

Knowing yourself is at the core of all defenses against Emotional Predators. Since ancient times, "know thyself" has been considered the source of all true knowledge. It's an insight and instruction attributed to many classical Greek scholars and to sources as far back as ancient Egypt. "Know thyself" was said to have been inscribed in the forecourt of the Temple of Apollo at Delphi where Pythia, the Delphic Oracle, lived.

Because Emotional Predators operate by knowing you better than you know yourself, *it's essential to reverse that situation and know yourself better than they know you.* The better you know yourself, the more effectively you can implement the defensive tactics described in Chapters 6 and 7. Learning about your unexamined assumptions, beliefs and core values protects you in many ways. It helps you recognize how you are undefended and how your habitual emotional reactions give an Emotional Predator ways to control you, and it lets you see Emotional Predators for what they are. It also helps you resist provocations, respond strategically, manage information, recover calm, immunize yourself, and regain control. We'll look at these things later in Part 2.

Knowing yourself better clears your vision in two principal ways. First it lets you see emotionally sensitive parts of yourself that are undefended and vulnerable to manipulation. An Emotional Predator will manipulate you by provoking emotional reactions from you, so you need to know the emotionally reactive buttons within you. Once you know them, you can start to conceal them. Eventually you can change your stories about yourself and the world to remove your emotional reactivity entirely. An Emotional Predator can't push an emotional button that you've hidden or eliminated.

Knowing yourself better also lets you see Emotional Predators for the manipulative abusers that they are. Your unexamined assumptions and beliefs distort your perceptions, making you gullible and blind to their charming facades. Knowing yourself limits the places they can hide among your distortions. A visible Emotional Predator is a weakened Emotional Predator.

So an essential line of defense is to uncover your own blind spots and emotional triggers. We all have blind spots - aspects of ourselves that we don't see. Emotional Predators count on that. *You can begin to get a glimpse of your blind spots when you look for issues, beliefs or situations that are emotionally charged for you.*[16] What are you passionate about, both as positive and as negative experiences? What brings you anger? Sadness? Joy? Despair? Hope? What do you pay attention to? What do you ignore? What do you avoid?

Because an Emotional Predators lives on provoking emotional reactions from you, it's vital to *avoid feeding him with your emotional reactions.* Provoking experience in you is a fundamental power he seeks both for its own thrill and for the information it provides about how to further manipulate you. So knowing yourself well enough to resist all provocations both keeps you invisible and starves the Emotional Predator for emotional reactions that tell him he's dominating you. Learning how you're susceptible to being provoked lets you shift from being emotionally reactive to being strategically responsive. Emotional reactivity leaves you vulnerable. Strategic responsiveness protects you.

Being strategically responsive instead of emotionally reactive empowers you with a number of tactics involving information. *Pretending to be oblivious* conceals the extent of your true knowledge and invites disclosures from the Emotional Predator. *Resisting the urge to respond* immediately or on his schedule restores power to you and disrupts his rhythms. *Misdirecting the Emotional Predator's attention* away from your emotional sensitivities protects what's important and vulnerable. *Documenting reality and his behaviors* supports your own sanity and provides you with ammunition to expose him, which at the right moment can be a powerful way to neutralize him.

The importance of being thoughtfully responsive, not emotionally reactive, can't be stressed enough. In addition to the strategic benefits, it helps you recover emotional calm from which you can rebuild after you've been targeted. So *monitor yourself* and watch your reactions carefully. Notice the conclusions you draw from your core values and assumptions - and be aware of the emotional reactions they elicit in you. When you notice you've become emotional about something involving an Emotional Predator, withdraw, regroup and take stock. *To be strategically responsive rather than emotionally reactive you have to be the adult in the room.* Adults know and manage their emotions, responsibly expressing them only when and how it's wise.

While an Emotional Predator will use any information about you to manipulate you, she'll make the most use of information about your emotions. *The more emotionally charged something is for you, the more closely connected it is to your sense of self, and the more easily you can be manipulated by it.* So an essential part of immunizing yourself is knowing your own emotional needs and discomforts better than she knows them. Your needs to be liked, adored, heard, respected and valued can create vulnerabilities - even an addiction - to an Emotional Predator. So can your fears, guilt, anger, shame and insecurities.

As you investigate yourself, particularly your emotional needs and things like your fears, guilt, anger, shame and insecurities, consider that emotional experiences are more within your control than you might think. We normally believe that we *have* these emotions, but it is more accurate to say these emotions have *us* - if we let them. For example, anger is most damaging to the angry person, but there are ways to transform anger.[17] Negative emotions like anger, blame and guilt are entirely optional. Don't opt for them. This takes practice so be kind to yourself.

You regain much control of your negative experiences when you stop making moral judgments of yourself. There's nothing to be gained, and lots to be lost, by indulging in moral judgments of yourself. *Instead of judging, observe yourself.* How strong are your needs to be liked, adored, heard, respected and valued? How do you use an Emotional Predator to feel better about yourself? Are you addicted to an Emotional Predator? It takes practice, but you can ask difficult questions about yourself without adding any moral judgments to whatever answers arise.

Past Emotional Injuries Create Present and Future Vulnerability

Each of us has our own unique history that creates individually specific ways an Emotional Predator can manipulate us. Investigating the specific emotional injuries you've suffered helps you develop something called "affect tolerance." Affect is a fancy word for emotion, so affect tolerance is the ability to tolerate the widest range and intensity of emotions. Because Emotional Predators leverage your emotional reactions to get what they want, affect tolerance is an essential element of protecting yourself. *The greater your ability to take things in stride and shrug off emotionally provoking things, the safer you are from Emotional Predators.* An Emotional Predator who can't trigger emotional reactions from you will move on to easier prey. Because your emotional triggers are automatic reactions generated from your personal history (clothed in beliefs you've adopted), it's useful to investigate the emotional pain you've been through and how it affects you now.

Pain can be emotional or physical. Physical pain can be emotionally painful as well (and emotional pain can lead to physical symptoms). Pain is a function of intensity over time. A short intense pain may be more bearable than a chronic mild pain. And a long term subtle infirmity can be as emotionally draining as a sudden injury. So whether pain you've suffered is chronic or acute, subtle or intense, and whether it's recent or in the distant past, knowing the contours of your own unique emotional history alerts you to your unique emotional vulnerabilities.

Generally speaking, pain that creates automatic future reactions in our nervous system is trauma, although the line between trauma and other emotional pain may not be clear. Among other things, trauma makes us hyper-reactive and easily provoked, things an Emotional Predator will leverage. For example, if you were beaten as a child, the threat of physical violence may trigger a cascade of physical and emotional trauma reactions in you. An Emotional Predator will use that to manipulate you by flashing anger to get you to comply. She can be like a dog who'll growl and snarl just enough to get you to back off.

There's no quick fix for serious trauma, and new treatments are developed from time to time, but the first step is to honestly investigate what you've been through and what reactions those experiences have embedded in your nervous system. Many trauma victims find it painful to look at this part of themselves, because recalling the memories in itself can be re-traumatizing. But facing your traumas is an important part of protecting yourself from further traumas at the hands of an Emotional Predator. And anyone who's been involved with an Emotional Predator for any length of time has been traumatized by the abusive nature of that relationship. If you've been traumatized, look into therapy with someone who's experienced helping trauma victims and consider a range of other help.[18] Different approaches work better for different people.

Emotional pain doesn't have to rise to the level of trauma to leave us reactive and easily triggered. Without realizing it, *many of us look to our adult relationships to try to overcome the disappointments of childhood*. This is natural, but can create problems. When we seek from adult relationships what we didn't get, or didn't get enough of, as a child, we risk at best falling into dysfunctional co-dependence, and at worst opening ourselves up to Emotional Predators. An Emotional Predator will quickly zero in on the messages you longed to hear as a child (and still do) and deliver those messages as part of seducing you. Typical messages we may not have heard enough from parents are things like "you're the most important person to me," "I want you to have what *you* want," "I'll always be here for you," "you're worthy of love just the way you are," and "you're more important to me than anyone else." Knowing what you long to hear to heal the injuries of your childhood alerts you to an Emotional Predator who's feeding you those messages to seduce you.

In addition to disappointments, you may have suffered affirmative injuries that aren't fully healed, or losses that aren't fully grieved, or both. These can be powerful emotional experiences that leave you vulnerable. Whether your disappointments and emotional wounds were suffered in childhood or later, the uncomfortable emotions they generate are a central part of yourself that you need to know better than an Emotional Predator can know them. When you avoid uncomfortable emotions, they don't disappear. They remain within you as powerful triggers to emotional reactivity, something Emotional Predators look for in potential targets. When you actively push away uncomfortable feelings, the situation gets worse. But things improve when you face them.

The Narcissistic Deficit and Blind Spots

As you look at your own emotional needs and blind spots, you may come up against *things you didn't get as a child*. Most people do. Put simply, almost everyone I know felt slighted or ignored or misunderstood (or worse) at some point during their childhood. These emotional injuries lead to what I call a "narcissistic deficit." Narcissism is over-used and misunderstood. A certain amount of narcissism (with a lower case n) - *attention to self* - is healthy. It becomes unhealthy and pathological Narcissism (with a capital N), when attention to self overrides attention to others. A narcissistic *deficit* happens when we don't get enough positive attention to our inner world when we were children.

All children need a certain type of attention from their parents. Beyond just acceptance, children need appreciation, respect and unconditional love in order to grow into mature, emotionally strong adults. Children need their parents to be genuinely curious about their unique inner child's world, an inner world that's different from (thus should be fascinating to) the parent. This kind of parental mirroring helps the child develop an honest and accurate sense of himself. Without it, the child develops a narcissistic deficit: a lack of healthy self-love.

Sigmund Freud said, "We demand reparation for the early wounds to our narcissism, our self-love." When the important parent-child relationships weren't enough about the child, as the child becomes an adult she tends to *compensate* for that deficit in one of two opposite ways depending on her capacity for empathy. People with impaired empathy who suffer a narcissistic deficit tend to become selfish Emotional Predators (a.k.a. Narcissists); the key parent relationships were not enough about them as a child, so as an adult they make relationships *all about them*.

But for empathetic people who suffer a narcissistic deficit, the response is more complex. Empathetic children intuitively understand that their parents aren't there for them because their parents are preoccupied with their own unmet needs. So empathetic children try to meet their parent's needs, hoping to heal their parent so their parent can be there for them. (Some call this the "parentified child" syndrome, because the child takes on the parent's role of meeting the other person's needs.) Empathetic people with a narcissistic deficit tend to become doormats; the key parent relationships were not enough about them, so as an adult they make relationships *all about the other person* and try to fill *the other person's* narcissistic deficit. Doormats seek out Emotional Predators (with narcissistic and other features) and try to *fix* or heal them.

So people who didn't get enough of the attention they needed as children seek to fill their own narcissistic deficit in opposite ways, depending on their innate empathetic sensitivity. The person with impaired empathy tries to make himself the center of all relationships. If that isn't a passing adolescent phase, these folks become Emotional Predators.[19] On the other hand, the empathetic person tries to heal the narcissistic deficit of the *other* person in the vain hope that this will enable the other person to reciprocate. If that isn't a passing adolescent phase these folks become doormats. The empathetic person is there for the other person, which makes them easy for an Emotional Predator to walk on. Doormats want to fix Emotional Predators, which is a hopeless mission. Emotional Predators want to walk on others to feel important, which is dangerous to others.

Another way to describe the opposite responses to a narcissistic deficit is that an Emotional Predator compensates with a *superiority complex*, and a doormat compensates with an *inferiority complex*. People going through an adolescent phase can bounce back and forth between inferiority and superiority responses, particularly when they're learning to supply themselves with the attention and respect they didn't get as a child (rather than seek it from a surrogate for their parent). And for all of us, *growing up demands that we fill our own narcissistic deficits and supply to ourselves the accurate mirroring we didn't get as children.*

Doormats and Emotional Predators tend to seek relationships with each other. Both use the other person in relationships as a surrogate for the parent they didn't have, first seeing the other person as the good parent they didn't have, then struggling with the other person as a stand-in for the bad parent they did have. An Emotional Predator will seduce a doormat with a false pitch that it's all about the doormat. Once the doormat is hooked, the Emotional Predator will make it all about herself, and the doormat will try in vain to repair the Emotional Predator. So, *failing to know your own narcissistic deficit creates a huge relationship blind spot.*

If you tend to be a doormat, which is a way of saying a target for Emotional Predator abuse, then it's important to learn about your own narcissistic deficit, and begin to *supply to yourself the appreciative attention you lacked as a child* - and to stop looking for a stand-in for your parent to supply it for you. It's never too soon to start giving yourself the positive attention and unconditional love that you missed as a child, instead of seeking it from an Emotional Predator.

So as part of knowing how past emotional injuries leave you vulnerable, recognize if you didn't get enough acceptance, appreciation, mirroring and unconditional love when you were young, leaving you with a narcissistic deficit and an inaccurately negative sense of yourself. That kind of negative self-esteem leads to self-victimizing beliefs such as: "if I only try a little harder or give a little more, then the Emotional Predator in my life will start meeting my needs." The section of this chapter about *Self-victimizing Beliefs* looks in more detail at these and other similar beliefs.

It's beyond the scope of this book to describe all the ways people have found to heal their own narcissistic deficits and emotional wounds. For example, to grow out of a doormat inferiority complex, you may need to *grieve* the lack of positive attention and unconditional love that you suffered as a child, instead of seeking those things from someone else. For our purposes, it's enough to recognize the feelings your narcissistic deficit generates, and to skip moral judgements of yourself about it. Your guilt, anger, shame, fears and insecurity are openings to Emotional Predator abuse.

When you face your pain and fears, you begin to be able to let them go. Letting them go opens new ways of being that are insulated from manipulation and abuse. There are many routes to transforming your unique losses, frustrated hopes and desires, and emotional pain - and to thus take yourself out of a cycle of automatic emotional reactions. Later in this chapter, the section about *Ways to Know Yourself Better* mentions some of them.

The hard news is that your adult relationships can't give you what you didn't get as a child or heal your emotional injuries, and seeking those things in adult relationships risks co-dependent addictive relationships - the kind that Emotional Predators foster and use. The good news is that you can deliver those things to yourself. Loving and forgiving yourself and delivering to yourself the messages you've sought from others is a potent way to immunize yourself from Emotional Predator manipulations. *Start by applying what I call the Golden Rule Turned Inward: treat every part of yourself the way you would like to be treated. If you like to be respected, valued, appreciated, nourished, considered, listened to and loved by others, then respect, value, appreciate, nourish, consider, listen to and love yourself.*

Respect, nurture and love all of your dreams, your ideas, your feelings, your physical states, and even your fears, shortcomings and insecurities. When you notice unpleasant aspects of yourself, negative self-talk and self-victimizing beliefs, don't attack yourself for them. Smile at them, thank them for getting you through earlier struggles and let them go. When you treat yourself poorly, you signal to others to do the same. So treat every aspect of yourself - the good, the bad, and the ugly - the way you want others to treat you.

KNOW WHAT IS CLOSEST TO YOUR HEART - RESIST YOUR DESIRE TO SHARE IT

The things you hold dearest and closest to your heart are things an Emotional Predator will leverage against you. Often the things closest to your heart are so close you don't see them clearly or even notice them. Your fears and hopes, your romantic desires and fantasies, your financial dreams, your unconscious assumptions and beliefs about yourself and others, and the things that gratify and feed your Ego are all things an Emotional Predator will quickly learn about you.

We can summarize these things as your *core beliefs and values – the stories you live by.* An Emotional Predator relies on knowing your core beliefs and values better than you know them. So protection requires reversing that and knowing these things about yourself better than he does.

Recognizing that an Emotional Predator will use your core beliefs and values to manipulate you doesn't mean you have to abandon them. Knowing your operative stories opens up a wider range of alternative stories that you can choose for yourself in different situations. It gives you more control over what you allow an Emotional Predator to know about you, which lets you strategically misdirect his attacks toward things that aren't important. In Chapter 7, we'll explore in detail ways to control information.

It takes courage and humility to recognize that your beliefs and values are *choices* based on assumptions. Start by *taking an inventory of your current beliefs and values*. One way to do this is to look at the stories you accept as "facts" about who someone is or who you think they *should* be, and about yourself and who you think *you* should be. But bear in mind that we can never know our self or someone else completely. There's always more to learn, so be patient and forgiving of yourself when you notice you've overlooked or misread something.

There are many ways to gain self-knowledge and many spiritual and psychological practices can help. No one way works well for everyone. A good therapist can help you uncover beliefs you don't realize you hold, acting as a mirror to show you things that are hard to see on your own. A good meditation practice can help you develop the patience to observe the contents of your mind without judgment or censorship, which is a good way to see the full range of things you believe and value. Use any practice that expands your knowledge of yourself.

As you take inventory of your operative stories, it's important to *resist the urge to let an Emotional Predator know what you discover* about yourself. "In relationship, it's good to be open and honest" is a core belief embedded in many modern relationship theories that can lead to disaster with Emotional Predators. Whether you're dealing with truths you discover about yourself or reality, or with insights you gain into an Emotional Predator, it's best to *know it, don't show it*. As you resist the urge to let an Emotional Predator know what you know, ask yourself why it feels important to let her know. That question leads you to see values and beliefs you hold that drive you to reveal too much.

For example, you may believe that displaying or showing off what you know will impress or intimidate others, or gain you respect and appreciation. While that might be true with some people, it won't be true with an Emotional Predator. Displaying or showing off what you know to an Emotional Predator just gives her information to use to manipulate you. So, when dealing with an Emotional Predator, it's important to not reveal too much, but instead to share only what would be strategically useful for protecting yourself and your loved ones. And, as we'll see in the section of Chapter 7 about *Set the Rules of Engagement*, at times you might be wise to share *misinformation* - untruth - that focuses her on manipulating things that don't affect you.

Thinking about being untruthful to an Emotional Predator may conflict with a core belief many of us hold: *the unquestioned belief that good people are always fully truthful.* This core belief - that it's important, good and responsible to be fully truthful - was drilled into most of us as children. But it can be particularly dangerous when dealing with an Emotional Predator. So consider that *being factually truthful is not the same as being situationally honest.*[20]

Because our thoughts and feelings flow faster than we can find words to express them, it's not possible to share everything we think and feel. This means that we're always disclosing only a selection of what's in our heart and mind. You can't help making choices about what to reveal and what to keep private; it's inevitable and natural. Selectively disclosing your thoughts, feelings and information might remind you of the Emotional Predator tactic of lying by omission. But Emotional Predators selectively disclose in order to manipulate others for their own ends. Keeping things to yourself *out of consideration for another or to protect yourself* is not the same. One way to tell the difference is to look at the underlying reason for keeping something private and the impact on innocent people.

The idea that factual truthfulness is different from emotional or situational honesty can be confusing. Imagine walking into the hospital room of a dear friend in the final stages of a terminal illness. Your friend looks terrible. The room smells of death. Your friend opens his eyes, struggles a faint smile and asks, "How do I look?" The *factually* truthful response would be something like "you look terrible, and it smells like death in here." But a *situationally* honest response might be something like "I've seen you looking better, but you always look good to me. It's always good to see you." Factual truth can be brutal. Situational honesty serves the well-being of innocent and good people.

Because Emotional Predators use information about you to manipulate you, it often serves the needs of the situation to *not* be fully truthful with an Emotional Predator and to hold your cards close and out of sight. *You wouldn't tell an opposing army's general where you've stored your weapons and supplies or how your defenses are organized, and you shouldn't tell an Emotional Predator what you know about yourself, her and the situation.* That doesn't make you dishonest. It makes you prudent, both when you're dealing with a confirmed Emotional Predator and also in situations where you aren't sure if someone is an Emotional Predator. It's wise to be cautious, resisting the good-hearted urge to treat a person of unproven trustworthiness as you'd treat a proven safe confidant.

And any time we choose to reveal something, we also must choose *how and when* to express it. These choices of what, how and when to share what's in our hearts and minds can further valuable ends or be damaging - to ourselves and to others. The Emotional Predator has mastered the arts of saying only certain things, in ways and at the times, that create the impression he wants - and using those arts to serve his own selfish ends. He's expert at lying by omission and innuendo from tone. Learn those arts to defend yourself. Rather than being an open book to satisfy an unexamined belief that you should always be totally truthful, be strategically selective about what, how and when you share with an Emotional Predator. This is explained in detail in Chapter 7.

When you think about keeping your personal information private from an Emotional Predator, be aware that *the questions you ask and the requests you make can reveal what's important to you*. If you ask an Emotional Predator lots of questions about finances and money, you're telling him that money is important to you. If you ask about your children's school, teachers and classroom activities, you're telling him that your children's education is important to you. So, if money is important to you but you're confident your children's education is well protected, consider asking lots of questions about your children's education, with the fewest possible about money randomly thrown in. The Emotional Predator would likely take the bait and waste his time and energy attacking you about the children's education. And if your children's education is important to you but you're confident that your finances will be fine, consider asking lots of questions about money, and randomly throwing in a few asides about their education. Whenever possible, *it's useful to misdirect the Emotional Predator's attention and energies to things that aren't important to you.*

The most important information to withhold is information about your emotions. To reduce the emotional information you release, and your overall emotional engagement, try pretending that you're a simple computer programmed to use the fewest possible words in your communications. Wherever possible, eliminate adjectives and adverbs, the words that carry most of the emotion in communication. Even if it feels like you sound comatose, adopt a bland, neutral tone in your writing - and in your tone of voice if you're audible, and in your facial expression and body posture if you're visible. A near monotone deadpan is a good tone for communicating with an Emotional Predator. For an example of a monotone style of speaking, watch some YouTube clips of comedian Steven Wright.

Confronted with no emotional expression and engagement from you, an Emotional Predator may initially ramp up her attempts to provoke you. If you don't take the bait, eventually she'll look elsewhere for someone to torment. And her ramped up attempts to provoke will make her true nature more visible to you and others, which is always good for you. As we'll explore in detail in Chapter 6, disengaging logistically and emotionally is a very strong first line of defense. And as we'll see in Chapter 7, if you must, or you choose to, remain engaged on a practical level, disengaging emotionally is a potent and necessary defense.

Other Desires That Can Betray You

Most of us share some basic human desires, things like the desire to be heard, included, loved and appreciated, and to live in a safe world of good people. With these and all desires, we become vulnerable to emotional manipulation when we focus on *the gap between what is and what we want*. The situation we're in, as they say, is what it is. But we often torment ourselves by comparing the way things are to a "better" alternative universe that we can imagine, but doesn't actually exist - and blaming ourselves for that gap. "Woulda, coulda, shoulda" messages of regret and self-criticism become ways to feel bad about yourself, even guilty, ashamed, depressed or anxious. Those negative feelings are undefended openings for Emotional Predators who will fan the fires of self-blame and self-denigration to weaken you. It never helps to dump on yourself, or as it's also called, "should" on yourself (scolding yourself for what you "should" have done or said).

The antidote to feeling down because of the gap between reality and an imaginary better world is to either focus your attention on what's good and right with your life *as it is*, or imagine an alternative life that would be *worse* than your life as it is, or both. Arlo Guthrie made a macabre joke of this by pointing out that it always makes you feel a little better to know there's someone else who has it worse than you.[21] *Rather than regret for what isn't, chose appreciation and gratitude for what is.* And that choice to feel grateful is always available to you; it's a matter of where you focus your attention. Even when you're enduring difficult even horrible things, you always have positive things to be grateful for. (Practicing gratitude is explained in more detail in Chapter 5) You can control your imagination and attention. Use it to help, not hinder, you.

When you think about your desires, it helps to distinguish between desires and needs. Many of the things you think you *need* are really just things you *want*. Needs are fairly simple: things like food, water, shelter, medical care, and some human intimacy and connection (although some folks can go a long time without some of these). It's natural to mislabel our wants as "needs" because it's hard to fault someone for going after what they need. So mislabeling something as a need can be a way to justify pursuing what you want - perhaps even to dodge guilt and responsibility for letting your consumerism and greed drive you at the expense of others.

Deceiving yourself by believing you need things that you actually only want is dangerous because it offers an Emotional Predator more "needs" to use as leverage. But recognizing that you really only want something that you'd thought you needed gives you more freedom of choice - and freedom from manipulation. So reduce the leverage an Emotional Predator can apply by shrinking the list of things you need. You may be able to do without more than you've thought possible, and feel better in the process. A gifted friend in his sixties was quite content to sleep on the floor of his studio so his son could use his house. He didn't need the comforts of his home and bed to feel fine. In terms of your needs and wants, consider whether less may be more.

Our desire to be heard and understood expresses the legitimate need for human connection. Without validation of how things are for us, it's easy to feel isolated and lonely, feelings an Emotional Predator will manipulate. This is particularly true when you've been through traumatic or confusing experiences, perhaps even from having been previously targeted by an Emotional Predator - and being targeted by an Emotional Predator is almost always highly traumatic and confusing. So someone who's been abused can be easy prey for a new abuser, who'll key into the abused person's need to be heard and understood about the abuse they've been through. As we've seen, it's dangerous to share personal things with an Emotional Predator.

Closely linked to the desire to be heard and understood are various forms of the desire to be liked and included. It's natural to want positive regard from others, to be respected, admired, adored or pursued. The old Cheap Trick song lyric says this well: "I want you to want me, I need you to need me." And the desire to be liked is an expression of our drive to be included in a group. We all naturally want to be included, to feel part of a group of like-minded people. There's safety in groups, *if* you are on the inside - and exclusion from a group is a potent torment for most primates. An Emotional Predator knows the power of groups, so he'll work hard to make you feel that doing what he wants is the way to feel safely on the inside, and that not doing what he wants will make you an outcast, a pariah, or just generally viewed as weird by your peers.

Most of us become finely tuned to being "in" or "out" as school children through peer pressure. You need only look as far as the nearest high school to see how the threat of exclusion is a powerful tool of manipulation. We like to pretend that peer pressure disappears as we become adults. But for many of us, peer pressure doesn't disappear with adulthood, it goes underground in the form of the social norms we adopt without question. An Emotional Predator uses peer pressure by telling you, or just implying, that all your friends (or everyone who matters) are doing what the Emotional Predator wants you to do, or that "everyone" will think badly of you if you don't do what he wants. So notice when someone applies peer pressure to manipulate you and recognize the group myths you buy into without realizing it, in particular myths that threaten social exclusion if you don't conform.

Social myths can be as invisible to us as the air we breathe, so to free yourself, first take an honest look at the conventions you assume you must follow. Then, "do what you will, laugh at convention. It's not a crime."[22] When you reject the social myths that keep you stuck in an Emotional Predator's web, your range of possible responses expands. And when you go your own way, rather than being socially isolated and excluded, you find new friends and new groups of like-minded people who value independent thinking, accountability, compassion, empathy and decency. There are plenty of safe and supportive groups open to you. You might be surprised by how many people connect over shared experiences of being targeted by Emotional Predators.

Although you may be actively working to re-balance power, don't become attached to a power struggle and your own desire to "win." *Your desire to feel yourself winning and dominating is one Emotional Predator game you do not want to play.* Being prideful is an easily overlooked way to let Emotional Predators provoke you. So don't let your pride skew your judgment and make you reactive. When you let go of your Ego need to win and you stay unprovoked, you can marshal your emotional and financial resources and wait for the most productive time to take action, rather than being drawn into battle by every obstacle and provocation. You don't need to win. It's enough to protect yourself and your loved ones. So don't compete. To paraphrase Joe Kennedy, Sr. (the father of President John F. Kennedy), don't get mad, get the *protection* that you and your loved ones need. Or as Pauli Murray put it "don't get mad, get smart."

Another desire many of us share is the desire to live in a safe world of good people, where others can be trusted to be kind and selfless. This is a beautiful desire and one I hope we all work to realize.

But as long as there are Emotional Predators, it's wise to be realistic and prudent. When you accept that some people aren't safe, your loss of innocence can be both a wound and a relief. In the film *Blue Velvet*, when the young man Jeffery (played by Kyle MacLachlan) realizes the true psychopathic nature of the character Frank (played by Dennis Hopper), he cries out in despair, "Why do there have to be people like Frank in the world?". The movie is the dramatic story of Jeffery's transition from naive to mature in his understanding of the types of people that exist, and his accepting responsibility for defending himself and others, even to the point of using the psychopath's weapon (in the movie, the weapon was a gun) against the psychopath.

A key element of the Emotional Predator's tactic of gaslighting is to make the target question their own sanity. So in response, when you're dealing with an Emotional Predator you naturally can feel a strong desire to expose and unmask him. Speaking and hearing the truth helps you stop feeling crazy in the face of his distortions. And if you grew up in a family where the truth wasn't well respected, then your desires to be validated, approved of, agreed with and appreciated can be very strong. Seeking validation of your experience with a *safe* person is cathartic and healing. But seeking validation from an Emotional Predator by trying to unmask him to himself is very dangerous; it provides rich material that he'll use to refine his manipulations. This reinforces the importance of identifying the Emotional Predators in your life and not being deceived by their facades, and of knowing who is genuinely safe to confide in.

Telling an Emotional Predator the negative things you see about him instructs him how to better hide his true nature, and may provoke anger and retaliation. Telling an Emotional Predator anything you know or believe teaches him how to better manipulate you. It's dangerous and foolish to believe an Emotional Predator will hear your truth, appreciate it and change. He won't have compassion for you. He won't see the error or indecency in his ways. He won't see how he's been distorting reality. And regardless of what he might notice about his behaviors, he won't care about how you suffer from them. He'll only care about how effective his behaviors are at getting him want he wants. So as we've seen and will touch on again, it's essential to control information by being strategic about what you share and with whom.

Distinguishing Romance from Mature Loving

Emotional Predators make powerful use of our romantic desires when they seduce and hypnotize us. Most people I know want to feel cherished, valued and loved. Much of our economy is driven by selling romantic hopes for getting these things. When she is laying a trap for you, an Emotional Predator will appear to completely adore you, to deeply share your world, to give you shelter from the storm and to be everything you've always dreamed of. Once you're hooked and committed, your dream person will become your worst nightmare. This is a good reason to *distinguish romantic love from mature loving*.

Despite the relentless advertising and marketing messages of our mercantile culture, *romantic love can be very dangerous*. Some years ago, a therapy group I ran called me the "romance dream killer" because of my concern about the dangers of romance. It's said that "love is blind" for good reason. Emotional Predators prey on the blindness of others, particularly the blindness induced by romantic love. To protect yourself, you need clear vision, not blindness.

The dangers of romantic love become clear when we understand that the romantic experience of "falling in love" *is a form of blinding ourselves* in order to try to master painful experiences from childhood. I call this the *mastery theory* of romantic love. As we've seen, Emotional Predators tune into your unmet needs from childhood that you seek to fulfill in adult relationships, and they hook you with a facade that they'll deliver those things. So it's important to understand the mastery theory of romantic love to recognize what you unconsciously seek when you fall in love.

The mastery theory of romantic love holds that there are no perfect childhoods. Everyone I know had some negative experiences with parent figures in childhood. The common element in all of these negative childhood experiences was that, because we were children, *we had no power to change them.* The mastery theory of romantic love says that, as adults we unconsciously seek out relationships that will re-create some aspect of those negative experiences. This sounds pretty dismal, but the mastery theory also says we do this not to relive those negative experiences over and over, but *to overcome them* - to gain *mastery* over them.[23]

Understood in light of the mastery theory, falling in love is the process of seeking out a partner who will re-create negative childhood experiences (so that we can eventually overcome those experiences). In order to get into an adult relationship that will re-create something negative from your childhood, you have to *blind* yourself to the negative traits in the other person that remind you of your childhood - traits that you're actually there to try to overcome.

Suppose Julie's father always told her that she had nothing worthwhile to say. As an adult, Julie attends a party where two men talk to her; one's a great listener and one's a lousy listener. Although it seems backwards, if Julie hasn't resolved her childhood wound of being told she had nothing worthwhile to say, she'll be captivated by the poor listener and will hardly notice the good listener. This is romantic "falling in love" starting to operate. Julie's unconscious blocks out the negative traits of the poor listener, leaving only positive traits in her awareness. In this highly filtered experience of him, he seems perfect and the honeymoon stage of romance begins.

Julie's unconscious continues this selective attention - this blinding - until she's gotten involved with the bad listener. She needs to get involved so she can try to overcome his poor listening trait that recreates her childhood wound. The honeymoon begins to wear off as her unconscious slowly lets that trait into her awareness - a trait that was in him all along. And that gives her the opportunity to stand up to and master her childhood injury, using him *as a surrogate for her father*. In this example, after Julie has been involved with the poor listener for some time she'll start demanding that he listen to her and take her seriously, and will be frustrated when he doesn't. The point for our purposes is to be aware of how romantic love blinds us in ways that make us vulnerable to Emotional Predators. An Emotional Predator will tune into your un-mastered childhood wounds, and pretending to be the person who'll heal them, will feed your blind romantic fantasies.

By contrast with romantic love, *mature loving isn't something we feel, it's something we do.* It's a way of selfless acting toward another who can reciprocate (unless they're a child or other innocent). Sadly, too often when someone says "I love you" they mean "I'm getting what I want from you," not "I want you to have what you want and need even if that means I won't get what I want and need." You can be confident that when an Emotional Predator says she loves you, no matter how desperate you are to hear that, what she's saying is that she's getting, or thinks she can get, what she wants from you. Remember, *no matter how intoxicating it feels, romance is not mature intimacy.* Cynical as it may sound, when you're involved in a passionate romance it's a time to be particularly vigilant about noticing signs of an Emotional Predator. Not all romance involves an Emotional Predator, but romantic love is a favorite stalking ground for Emotional Predators.

Self-victimizing Beliefs

Sometimes the stories you tell yourself about who you are and who you must be in order to be a "good" person can trap you and leave you undefended. Usually without noticing, we all inhabit stories about who we have to be in order to be lovable, valued and safe with others. We usually adopt these stories from our families and culture, though each of us can re-write them in our own distinctive way. When these stories put us in a one-down or vulnerable position in relation to others, I call them our "self-victimizing beliefs." *Self-victimizing beliefs make a person low hanging fruit for Emotional Predators.* I'll introduce some of these stories here, and in Chapter 5, we'll revisit some in more detail as we look at *Alternatives to a few Common Stories.*

One self-victimizing belief many of us are familiar with is the belief that "I'm not good enough." This mistaken belief is an expression of *perfectionism.* A perfectionist believes that if he isn't perfect, everything is his fault. Like focusing on bad things or on good things that are missing, instead of being grateful for good things that are present, perfectionism depends on the perspective you choose. Put another way, the perfectionist hasn't learned that "good enough" is good enough. He mistakenly sees himself as a slacker for whom "good enough" is *not* good enough. It isn't hard to see how an Emotional Predator could use your beliefs about not being good enough or needing to be perfect to induce guilt and shame to get you to comply with her agenda. She would let you know that you *could* be good enough (she may even say "perfect") if only you would do what she wants, dangling the carrot of approval just out of reach. But you're good enough without her; you don't need her unattainable approval. If you're a perfectionist, let yourself off the hook of perfectionism and know that "good enough" is actually good enough.

Another self-victimizing belief is a *martyr complex* in which we believe we have to suffer in order to feel worthy of love (or anything else we want). Like a doormat adaptation to a narcissistic deficit, a martyr type finds it easier to focus on other people than on himself. An Emotional Predator seeks out targets who'll focus on her at the expense of themselves. A martyr type believes that he'll be appreciated and valued for his sacrifices and that the person he sacrifices for will naturally want to reciprocate; he gives in the hope of getting back what he's giving. This makes him an ideal target for Emotional Predators (who are takers). If you recognize martyr tendencies in yourself, work to replace them with appreciation of your intrinsic and inherent worthiness, a worthiness that exists without needing to make sacrifices. Then choose to make sacrifices only when you know it'll be a two-way street and the other person gives as much as you do and doesn't just take.

Closely related to martyrdom, *confusing enabling with helping* is another belief that leaves us vulnerable to Emotional Predators. Enabling is taking responsibility for something another person is responsible for. It allows the other person to avoid the negative consequences of their poor choices. An enabler makes excuses for another person's bad behavior and believes the fiction that these excuses "help" the other person. Twelve step addiction recovery programs like Alcoholics Anonymous advise that, in order to help someone let them suffer the consequences of their own choices and find their own bottom, and to do otherwise is dangerous to them and you. Standing firm and not making excuses for others or taking up the slack when they slack off doesn't mean being harsh or unkind. Being kind doesn't mean tolerating abuse. Being a good person doesn't require being a sucker. But an Emotional Predator will work hard to convince you otherwise, playing on your conscience and guilt to get you to enable them. I try to help only people who take responsibility and have already done all they can for themselves.

People-pleasers are a type of enabler. They live by self-victimizing stories that put them in the role of making everything all right for everyone else. Roberta, a client of mine told me, with a mixture of pride and embarrassment, "I'm really good at figuring out what other people want and giving it to them. That's how I get everyone to like me." This sounds like what an Emotional Predator will do. The difference is she did this at great cost to herself, not to her own benefit, putting everyone else's needs ahead of her own. In therapy, Roberta worked hard to change this story about what it takes for people to like her. And she wrote herself a new story that it's okay for her to pay attention to the cost *to her* of the things she does for others. Her new story didn't make her selfish, far from it. When self-sacrificing people first move a bit away from self-sacrifice and toward self-care, they often feel like they've become a selfish monster. But it only *feels* that way in comparison to their prior overly self-sacrificing ways. If you're a self-sacrificing people-pleaser, shift your focus away others and give your own feelings and needs more priority.

One sign of people-pleasing is feeling like you have to explain or justify your boundaries and needs. Another is easily yielding to social pressure. We've touched on the exceptionally strong need to feel part of a group that makes teenagers particularly susceptible to people-pleasing in the form of peer pressure. Another sign of people-pleasing is always playing the clown or entertainer, or always diffusing tensions. People-pleasers relentlessly avoid conflict. Conflict avoiders believe a story that conflict between people is always bad and that it's their job to do anything and everything to eliminate all conflicts, regardless of the cost to them. They'll always back down and accommodate, and if necessary, take blame. All these things make people-pleasers easy targets for Emotional Predators.

Some common self-victimizing stories come from religious or church affiliations. I worked with a man whose church condemned divorce. His wife had been diagnosed as a sadistic psychopath by several psychiatrists and psychologists. She repeatedly beat him up and spent their savings on junkets with other men. But, because he was deeply afraid of displeasing the church elders who didn't approve of divorce and told him that every marriage problem was the husband's fault and responsibility to fix, he kept himself trapped with her abuse. He was abused and felt guilty for it. His church leaders blamed him for any problem in his marriage, in my view completely misunderstanding the nature of the problem and making it worse. He finally let go of that church's story that a godly man would never leave his wife and that he should keep giving her "love and understanding," no matter what she did, and switched to another less controlling denomination. By opening himself up to a new religious story, he was able to divorce her and protect himself and his children.

A few other commonly held beliefs - myths of our culture - that can be self-victimizing bear mentioning. It's widely believed that we can *cause* other people to feel the emotions they feel. This belief is embedded in our language. We regularly say, "You make me feel" this or that. But this isn't true. The emotions a person feels are generated *by that person* out of the assumptions and interpretations he makes about the meaning of events. Two people faced with the same circumstance can have opposite emotional reactions: one laughs while the other cries.

For example, a stranger yells at two people standing at a bus stop minding their own business. One of them bursts into tears because he interprets the yelling to indicate something bad about *himself*. He believes that people don't yell at others without good reason, so when he's yelled at he concludes that he must've done something wrong or there must be something wrong with him. He assumes he must be at fault because a stranger is yelling at him. But the other person bursts into laughter, not tears, because she interprets the yelling to indicate something bad about the *yeller*. She assumes there's something wrong with a person who yells at a stranger. Each person's feelings are generated by how they *choose* to interpret events; they aren't caused by someone else. Emotional Predators will use guilt to manipulate you by telling you that you're "making" them feel bad. Don't believe it. Act responsibly and let others take responsibility for their feelings.

Another culturally popular self-victimizing belief is that *altruism toward all* is always a good thing. An altruist meets someone else's needs without regard for her own; she selflessly puts the other person first. Altruism is one of the most noble and valuable capacities of human beings. But it's a disaster to be altruistic toward an Emotional

Predator. An Emotional Predator will take advantage of an altruist in every imaginable way, and will present false needs and plays for sympathy to keep the altruist giving, giving and giving, while getting nothing back. I've never met anyone with an inexhaustible capacity to give without getting anything back (although martyrs try). Exhausting your altruistic instincts on an Emotional Predator means you have less resources left to altruistically give to genuinely deserving people.

Another self-victimizing cultural myth that opens the door to Emotional Predator abuse is the belief that good things happen to good people who work hard. This is a very commonly held belief, with roots in the protestant work ethic and capitalism. This *meritocracy myth* burdens its believers with unnecessary guilt and shame from its unspoken inverse; if we believe that good things happen to good people who work hard, then bad things must happen to bad people who are lazy. When we believe the meritocracy myth and a bad thing happens to us, we assume it's because we were bad or lazy or both. Buying into this myth leaves you open to Emotional Predator manipulation through guilt and shame. She'll create problems for you, then blame them on your supposed inadequacy.

In fact, life is much more random than we want to believe. Sometimes, bad things happen to good people who work hard and good things happen to bad people who are lazy. This doesn't mean life is completely random and beyond control. You can increase *probabilities* of good outcomes by working hard and being good, but you can't guarantee them. And being a good person with a work ethic yields internal rewards apart from external outcomes. But when bad things happen to you, it doesn't mean there's something wrong with you or you deserved it.

Freeing yourself from self-victimizing beliefs lets you take more responsibility for your own emotions while letting others be responsible for theirs. This increases your power and insulates you from Emotional Predator abuse. When you're more insulated from Emotional Predator abuse a few things happen: it becomes easier to conceal the emotional reactions you do have and to respond strategically, and your inner resources are less drained - all of which makes you a less inviting target.

As in all aspects of protecting yourself from Emotional Predators, you have much more power over your emotional reactions than you might believe. One person's disaster is another person's learning opportunity. Natural disposition, temperament and personal history no doubt play a part, but your *choices* of interpretation, perception and attention play the decisive role in determining whether you'll cry or laugh at the same thing. Let go of your self-victimizing beliefs and more control over your emotions will follow.

One way to spot our self-victimizing stories is to notice that *what we believe others require of us is usually a projection of what we require of ourselves.* When you believe you have to be perfect before someone else will love you, you're really expressing that you believe you have to be perfect before *you* will love yourself. If you believe in giving everyone the benefit of the doubt, you're really expressing that you want to give *yourself* the benefit of the doubt. If you believe you should try to see the good in everyone, then you're really expressing that you want to see the good in *yourself.* If you make excuses for others, then you're really expressing that you want to excuse *yourself.* If you make exceptions for others, then you're really expressing that you want to give *yourself* a break. The defense against all kinds of self-victimizing beliefs - the way to re-write self-defeating stories - is to deliver to yourself the things you believe others require from you and that you mistakenly seek from others. That isn't selfish. That's balanced and mature.

If you recognize any self-victimizing stories in yourself, try turning the Golden Rule inward and treat every aspect of yourself the way you'd like to be treated, and certainly treat yourself as well as you treat anyone else. *If you deliver to yourself the things you mistakenly seek from others, then Emotional Predators can't manipulate you by pretending to offer those things to you.*

OTHER THINGS TO KNOW ABOUT YOURSELF

Other things to know about yourself are *how you react under stress*, and *what you do to de-stress and restore a sense of safety*. In many situations, your habitual reactions do temporarily restore a feeling of safety, which is why you developed them in the first place. But with an Emotional Predator, they can sabotage you and make you predictable in ways that don't serve you in the long run. He will put you under stress to get you reacting in automatic ways, and then accuse you of being the problem because of your reaction.

When stressed or threatened, do you engage or do you withdraw and retreat? Do you entertain, becoming the life of the party? Do you redouble your efforts? Do you appease, justify and make excuses for others? Do you try to figure things out or do you fall back on your gut instincts? Do you talk or get quiet? Do you get lost in details (losing the forest for the trees), or fail to pick out relevant details (losing the trees for the forest)? Do you defer to others and seek advice, or do you hunker down with what you already believe? Whatever your particular habitual style of reacting to stress and danger, an Emotional Predator will quickly know it and use it to manipulate you. So knowing how you habitually react under stress and threat allows you to choose more strategically wise responses.

A single mother allowed others to mistreat her. When she was stressed, she'd make excuses for others and redouble her efforts to do more and more. Her ex-husband was an Emotional Predator who knew her stress response style and played it to her disadvantage over and over. He set up a parenting schedule for their two young children so he only had them part of two weekends a month and one weekday afternoon every other week, leaving him free to party with his new girlfriend. The mother was left with her job and ninety-five percent of the parenting responsibility. She'd make excuses for why she couldn't take him to court to change that schedule and collect the child support he didn't pay, which forced her to work every free moment to make ends meet.

The few times that he did take the children were her only chance for rest. He knew this (because she would tell him) and would purposely pick them up as much as two hours late, without texting or calling to let her know when he'd actually arrive (a textbook display of passive aggression). She'd have the children all ready to be picked up at the correct time, and they'd wait and wait and wait. This would ruin any plans she might have made for the already limited time of her break from parenting.

When he didn't show up on time, her habitual reaction was to become frazzled and incoherent and to start mindlessly tidying up, which got more intense the longer she waited. Instead, if she had just waited fifteen minutes and then left with the kids for a movie or something fun, simply by not being there when he eventually arrived she would've communicated that she wasn't controlled by his passive-aggression. And by keeping the children with her, she would've been using the Emotional Predator tactic of passive-aggression against him. But she just waited and waited, getting more and more stressed, and when he finally showed up, she displayed her stressed agitation to him - which he loved.

Having let him work her into a frenzy of frazzled agitation and then showing him how he had provoked this in her, when he finally took the children, she'd fall back on her "do more and more" stress response. With the little time she had left to herself before the children returned she'd labor with laundry and cleaning instead of taking a genuine break. The more frazzled she got, the less self-care she did, which made her more easily frazzled, which made her less and less able to be strategic and protect her need for self-care, which made her more and more emotionally reactive. She was a fraught mess, always with an excuse for why she "had to" do things the way she did them: not setting boundaries with her ex and not taking a genuine break when she could. When I gently observed these things to her, she got angry at me. (Attacking the messenger is a sign that someone is too reactive, at least in the moment, to summon up the self-awareness needed to protect themself.) Over time when she was able to calm down, she gradually gained more insight and adopted more protective responses to stress.

In addition to our particular habitual stress reactions, most of us deal with stress and emotional pain by *self-medicating* in some way. The "medication" in self-medicating refers to anaesthesia, something that provides relief from pain, a palliative. By *self*-medicating, I mean something we do to help our self feel better about things that are uncomfortable. Self-medicating manages the symptom of dis-ease we experience, but doesn't remedy the underlying causes. It's not a cure. Viewed psychologically, self-medicating is a form of repressing or pushing away from awareness things that are difficult to face. In simpler language, self-medicating is a form of escape.

There's nothing inherently wrong with self-medicating. Occasional and temporary relief from life's troubles is a good thing. It's not easy to be a person, and everyone I know does things - self-medicates - to feel better. The important question with respect to protecting yourself from Emotional Predators is whether the things you do to self-medicate *blind you to aspects of yourself* that an Emotional Predator will know and use against you. Self-medicating can block your awareness of three things: the underlying feelings you're avoiding, the means you employ to avoid, and how dependent you are on those means. So for protecting yourself, it's important to recognize what you do to self-medicate (the means), how much you do it, and what that prevents you from knowing about yourself (what we avoid).

Self-medicating can be confused with addiction. I don't define addiction as something you can't stop doing. I can't stop breathing or eating (and I do them to avoid discomfort), but that doesn't make them addictions. If what we do to self-medicate incurs *collateral consequences* that are too costly, it's an addiction. An addiction might be too costly to you or others, and others may have a different view of what is and isn't a cost. People near you might see aspects of your self-medicating as destructive and call it an addiction, but you may not see negative consequences and see it only as stress relief. In this view, addiction could be said to lie in the eye of the beholder.

Many ways of self-medicating can become an addiction: television, video screens, phones, social media, substances, risk taking, gambling, shopping, sex, career, exercise, diets and passions of all sorts. None of these are intrinsically good or bad. It's the negative collateral consequence of these "medications" that determines whether they're an addiction. If you work so much that your relationships suffer, if you exercise so much that you're constantly injured, if you diet so much that you're malnourished, if you eat so much that you're overweight, if you're on social media so much that you lose sleep, if you gamble away more money than you can afford - these are collateral consequences that can be too costly, pushing your relief activity over the line to being an addiction.

Again, for defending against Emotional Predators, the common dangerous consequence of all addictions is that they blind you to your uncomfortable feelings - and the beliefs and stories that generate those feelings. But those feelings remain within you, visible to and usable by an Emotional Predator, but not you. With respect to protection against Emotional Predators, if the collateral consequence of your self-medicating is to deny you access to your core beliefs and values and the operative stories of your life, then it's a very dangerous addiction.

And, of course, if you self-medicate with relationships or sex, you're particularly wide open to the manipulations of an Emotional Predator. Do you feel too unsafe or dependent to end a relationship? A client in an addictive relationship with an Emotional Predator told me "I couldn't tolerate it anymore. Something inside me was saying like a big 'No.' But I couldn't stop. I had to go back to him. I couldn't survive alone." As she realized that her attraction to him was an addiction, and part of a habitual reaction that masked deeply buried insecurities, she learned to find less destructive sources of security, which helped her survive and prosper without him.

I don't make light of the very real tragedy of addictions. I recognize that my ideas about addictions and stress relief invite the disapproval of many twelve-step and other traditional addiction theorists, whose programs have saved many, many people from devastating addictions. But in light of our exploration of the problem of Emotional Predators, three things bear noting. First, traditional approaches to addiction can create "no-win" binds for someone accused of being addicted. Second, in traditional approaches the accuser sets up the inquiry as an "either/or" question - either you are addicted or you are not - rather than as an inquiry into consequences in light of the full multi-faceted situation, including what the *accuser* may contribute to the stress from which the accused is seeking relief. And third, an accusation of addiction can be an emotionally compelling story based on partial facts.

Setting up no-win binds for others, viewing things as either/or, and telling emotionally compelling stories that leave out relevant facts are all common Emotional Predator tactics and traits. But seeing that an Emotional Predator is using an accusation of addiction as a form of abuse doesn't absolve the accused. As we've seen, a target of an Emotional Predator is responsible for his behaviors, even if he's been provoked or driven to them by her. "She drove me to drink" is never an excuse, although it can help us understand the true *interrelated* nature of the situation, and re-balance a false "victim/ perpetrator" story.

Here's how a traditional accusation of addiction sets up a "no-win" bind and sees things as either/or: the accuser takes "denial" to be a defining part of an addiction, so if the accused doesn't agree that he's addicted, the accuser sees his denial as "proof" of the addiction. Saying denial of an addiction *proves* the addiction is a meaningless trap. It's like the medieval practice of submerging people in water to determine if they're witches (called "ducking"). Wikipedia describes that practice this way: "The victim's right thumb was bound to her left big toe [so she could not swim or float flat]. A rope was attached to her waist and the 'witch' was thrown into a river or deep pond. If the 'witch' floated it was deemed that she was in league with the devil, rejecting the 'baptismal water'. If the 'witch' sank she was deemed innocent."[24] Either way, the accused was condemned. That's a no-win bind if ever there was one.

Practitioners of ducking as a way to prove witchcraft used fallacious arguments and theories to support their abusive practice. Some argued that witches floated because they'd renounced baptism when entering the Devil's service. King James VI of Scotland (later James I of England) claimed in his *Daemonologie* that water was so pure an element that it repelled the guilty, pushing them to the surface. These notions are as unscientific as the notion that denial of addiction confirms the addiction.

In the no-win bind of traditional addiction theory, if you deny you're an addict, it proves you're an addict, and if you accept the accusation of being an addict, then you're also an addict. Either way, *the accusation itself allows only one conclusion*. That's a false inquiry. A more useful, and honest, inquiry would be to ask what factors in a person's internal and interpersonal environments contribute to the behavior that's being labeled as "addictive," and what are the collateral consequences, both positive and negative. And of course, it's enlightening to ask *who* is deeming the collateral consequences of the behavior to be negative, and *what benefit the accuser gets from the accusation*. Claiming victimhood (in this case being the victim of the alleged addict), is a standard tactic of Emotional Predators.

To summarize about self-medicating and addictions, being a person can be hard from time to time, and we all do things to help us feel a bit better. When the collateral costs of those things are deemed to be destructive, they're called addictions. But when the collateral costs are deemed to be neutral or constructive, they're called things like hobbies, careers, diets, exercise routines, passions, art interests, stress relief, and relationships. Anything that we do can become destructive if carried too far. Exercise can lead to endless injuries. Jobs can lead to estrangement from family and friends. Diets can become eating disorders. Occasional wagers can become bankrupting gambling. Television and internet surfers and gamers can become sleep deprived and isolated. For defending against Emotional Predators, the most relevant collateral cost is limiting your ability to see yourself clearly, which opens you up to abuse and manipulation. And accusations of addiction can be an Emotional Predator's tool of domination and manipulation.

Sun Tzu was clear that having better information and controlling information is an essential aspect of winning a war. Because Emotional Predators operate by knowing you better than you do, you need to reverse the balance of power by coming to know yourself better than an Emotional Predator does. There are many things to know about yourself: your emotional vulnerabilities, the emotional injuries of your childhood (and after), your deepest fears, hopes and desires, your core values and beliefs, your habitual reactions to stress, your ways of self-medicating, the assumptions you make about yourself and others, the stories you live by. The next section looks at a few ways that people have come to know themselves better.

WAYS TO KNOW YOURSELF BETTER

There are many ways to learn about yourself. No single route or technique works for everyone or for one person at every stage of their life. Often it's best to combine many ways. Meditation, therapy, good books, sensory deprivation tanks, art, exercise, fasting, cooking, yoga, solitude in nature, group activities, psychedelics, physical challenges, social media breaks, and insights from trusted friends and family are some things my clients have used to learn about themselves. As you explore yourself, you may run into practitioners of a particular technique who believe that their way is the *only* way. They have a hammer, so they see everything as a nail. But no single technique fits everyone at every phase of their life and in every situation. Try different paths and see what works for you.

The common requirement for all ways of knowing yourself better is *courage*. When it comes to learning about yourself (and others and the world), don't fear the unknown and unfamiliar. If you come upon a steep cliff across your path of learning ... jump! It's not as far down as you think. And learning about your *fears* is one of the most useful things you can do.

As you seek to know more about yourself than an Emotional Predator knows about you, you may be unsure when to trust your gut feelings, intuition and thoughts. When are they clear messages about reality? When are they distorted expressions of your unresolved conflicts, emotions and beliefs? Put another way, when can you rely on your internal BS meter? Victims of domestic abuse can be convinced that they aren't doing enough for their abuser and feel guilty about causing the abuse they're suffering - thoughts and feelings disconnected from reality and generated by distortions from within.

Particularly if you've been gaslighted by an Emotional Predator but in other situations as well, knowing when you can trust yourself is a crucial question that can take time to answer.

This raises the foundational question of how we know what we know and what we can trust. That's a huge topic - epistemology - disputed by philosophers, theologians, psychologists and scientists for centuries. For our purposes, let's be practical and look at a few ways that I've seen clear the fog of distortion from people's perceptions. There are others.

Carl Jung described a framework for understanding how we know that I've found useful with many clients. With apologies to my Jungian colleagues, in broad brush strokes, according to Jung there are four different ways to know things, to gain information. He called them *functions of consciousness*. We improve our internal BS meter (Jung didn't use that term) when we develop each of these four ways so that we rely on all of them more or less equally. We create blind spots when we rely too much on some ways and not enough on others.

Jung's four ways of knowing are *thinking, feeling, sensation* and *imaging* (Jung called imaging "intuition" but imaging is more accurate)[25]. *Thinking* separates experience into parts and rearranges them in relation to each other. This is how grammar operates, putting subjects (actors), verbs (actions) and objects (the acted upon) into different relations with each other. *Feeling* is the moods we pick up on, including the extremes of mood that we call emotions. Emotions are particularly intense feelings, but feelings also include subtle experiences that might not rise to the level of emotions, like a sense of calm at dusk. *Sensations* are the physical feedback our body gives us. Chills, tightness in our chest and nausea are typical ways our bodies inform us. And *imaging* is the dream states we have both awake and asleep. These four ways of knowing are interconnected. Artists use images that evoke feelings and thoughts. Feelings can bring forth sensations, as when we're so upset we become sick to our stomach or it becomes hard to breath. Thoughts bring up feelings. Feelings bring up thoughts. And dreams include the other three.

Jung believed that *imbalance* among these four ways of knowing limits the accuracy of our understanding. Because our culture overvalues thinking, most of us tend to believe we ought to be able "figure out" what's what and what to do. If you're imbalanced in favor of thinking in this way, you can improve your internal BS meter by developing the other ways of knowing - feelings, sensations and images - so that you rely on them as much as you rely on your thinking. If you're imbalanced in favor of any of the four, developing those you don't naturally favor so that you rely on all four ways more or less equally will minimize distortions.

To re-calibrate your internal BS meter, there's no substitute for consulting people that you know are safe, uninvolved and decent people of conscience and courage. These people can be found in books and in person, and if you're discerning, on the Internet. But beware, the Internet is a playground for Emotional Predators, some of whom masquerade there as "helpers" and "experts." I've seen more than one site about psychopaths that I suspected were run by a psychopath, and many more that offered amateur, even dangerous, advice. On the other hand, the Internet does let you access experts beyond your local area via things like video conferencing, podcasts and webinars. As you look for people to consult, screen carefully. And remember that *your true friends are the folks who will risk telling you things about yourself and someone you're involved with that they think you don't want to hear.* When you're involved with an Emotional Predator, the truth is rarely comfortable to hear. And Emotional Predators will cut you off from others who would offer feedback you need.

Meditation is an ancient way to clear your mind of illusions and delusions. Many of my clients have found that meditating for just fifteen minutes a day changed their lives. One told me that Buddhist meditation trained her to not be taken over by her wants and desires, and to stay calm in her truth in the midst of swirling emotional provocations. There are many types of mediation practices and many resources available for learning how to develop a meditation practice. I find Thich Nhat Hanh's books to be accessible and simple to follow. Local meditation groups, tapes and even phone apps also can be good ways to learn mediation.

For all its varieties and intricacies, for our purposes meditating is really very simple. Briefly, to start meditating all you need is a comfortable seat and a timer. Sit comfortably, with your back straight and your feet squarely on the ground. Set a timer for five minutes. As you become more practiced, you can increase the time in five minute increments up to twenty or thirty minutes. Once you've set your timer, be as still as you can, ceasing bodily movements except for your breathing. In Zen style, your eyes are gently open, looking at the floor about three or four feet in front of your feet. In other styles, your eyes are closed.

Then all you do is bring your attention to your breathing and count your breaths from one to ten. When you get to ten, you start again at one. And if you notice that your mind has wandered to anything other than your breathing, smile internally at where it's wandered, gently return your attention to your breath, and re-start your count at one. When the timer goes off, you're done.[26] A devoted student of this meditation practice who later ran a Zen center told me that after decades of extended daily practice, if she was honest with herself, she never got beyond three in her count before her mind wandered and she returned to one.

The goal of this style of mediating isn't to get to ten. The goals are to improve concentration and awareness, with improved concentration leading to expanded awareness. First practice *concentrating your attention* on one thing (your breath). As you get more practiced at concentrating your attention, you begin to *become aware* of where your mind habitually wanders when it wanders (and it will wander). Increasing your awareness of your habits of mind can be life changing, particularly when you're learning about yourself to build protections against an Emotional Predator. As you expand your awareness, you see the assumptions, beliefs, stories and values you live by that you hadn't noticed before.

A good therapist also can be an invaluable tool for learning about yourself. If someone you know has changed in profound and positive ways, find out if they had help from a therapist and see if that therapist might be a good fit for you. But as we've seen, the mental health professions attract a disproportionate share of Emotional Predators, so be savvy about screening any therapist you consider. A therapist who doesn't fully understand Emotional Predators might still be able to help you learn what you need to know about yourself. But a therapist who doesn't know herself well or who plays the game of keeping herself hidden behind a screen of professionalism, theory or jargon isn't likely to be much use. And don't assume that a therapist knows more about Emotional Predators than you do. If you've read this book and the others listed in endnote 32, the odds are that you know more about Emotional Predators than most therapists.

To review Chapter 4, coming to know your core beliefs, values and assumptions, the stories you live by, specific things about your emotional history that leave you emotionally reactive and your habitual stress responses is vital for protecting yourself from Emotional Predators. Better knowledge of self clears your vision for spotting them. Better knowledge of self helps you know what feeds you and what drains you, information they will use to manipulate you. Better knowledge of self lets you replace emotional reactions with strategic responses.

An Emotional Predator will strive to know your weak places and attack you there. Unless you know your emotional vulnerabilities at least as well as he does, you can't know where you need to defend. So know your weak places, strengthen them and divert attacks away from them and toward your strong places. Later when we look at specific strategies for protecting yourself in Chapters 7, we'll look at ways to mislead an Emotional Predator to make your weak places appear strong and your strong places appear weak, to trick him into attacking where he can't prevail. Have the courage to learn about yourself, using whatever tools work best for you.

chapter five

Step 3 - How to be Flexible About the Ways You Define Yourself that Make You Vulnerable

You can change your vulnerabilities into defenses by being flexible about your core beliefs and assumptions - the stories you inhabit.

"We don't see things the way they are. We see things the way we are."
Anais Nin

THE POWER OF CHANGING YOURSELF

The last chapter looked at knowing how you are emotionally reactive and can be triggered by your core beliefs and stories about who you are and must be, and about what's happening around you. In this chapter, we'll look at how you can become less emotionally reactive and more strategically responsive by loosening your grip on those beliefs and stories and re-defining yourself. Emotional Predators seek out emotionally reactive people and harness their emotional reactions to control them. But a strategically responsive person can regain control and power, and is a less appealing target. Your emotional reactions control you. You control your strategic responses.

Although it's natural to want to change an Emotional Predator, don't underestimate the power of changing *yourself*. Knowing yourself better than she knows you is essential, but more powerful protection comes when you're willing to *change* yourself. And you're the only person you can change. You can't change who she *is*. You can, however, change who *you* are to fortify your defenses, build immunity and improve your responses. And by changing yourself and how you respond, you can influence her *behaviors*. Later we'll look at specific strategies to influence Emotional Predators' behaviors, but don't confuse that with changing *who they are*.

Relationships are dances; when one dance partner changes their steps, the dance itself changes. When you're dancing with an Emotional Predator, your toes are getting stepped on. But when you change yourself, your dance steps change. They might not improve right away, but at a minimum you get new data, which point to other changes to try. Whether it's with an Emotional Predator or elsewhere in your life, learning from change is a trial and error process. Think of changes you make as experiments, rather than as grasping for the "right" thing. Like a good scientist, keep an open mind, as free as possible from pre-judgment. The first step is to notice that the steps you've been dancing - the stories you live by - are choices you've made and that you can change your steps.

The way you are is much more the result of your choices than you might think. Whether you realize it or not, evolving and learning new stories to live by is a natural part of aging. To protect yourself from Emotional Predators, be willing to let go of who you have been and try on new ways of being you that are better protected. You have the freedom to choose what you believe and how you remember things - to pick the stories you inhabit, which create who you are. *You can choose to be someone less vulnerable to an Emotional Predator.*

So if you want protection from Emotional Predators, be flexible about your beliefs and willing to change. Don't believe everything you think and don't believe everything you believe. Loosen your grip on who you believe you are, on who you believe you must be with others, and on what you believe is going on in your world.

As you consider changing yourself, remember that it's natural to resist change. Changing yourself, like learning about yourself, takes courage. Fear of change is a form of fear of the unknown, which is almost always exaggerated. Keep in mind Albert Einstein's observation that insanity is doing the same thing over and over, and expecting a different result. And remember that failing to prepare is preparing to fail.

WE WRITE OUR STORIES - THEY CREATE OUR EXPERIENCE

We choose our stories - the beliefs we live by - and they create our experience. Many of the beliefs we treasure as sacrosanct today will be discarded in a hundred years (or sooner), as we've discarded beliefs from previous times and cultures. Sensible people today scoff at old beliefs like "disease can be cured by applying leaches" and "the earth is flat" and "the sun orbits the earth," but these were widely accepted as obvious "truth" in their day. *The unquestioned truths of years past are laughed at today, just as the obvious truths of today may well be laughed at in days to come.* It wasn't so long ago that "spare the rod, spoil the child" was widely accepted as good parenting. Today that's called child abuse.

As we saw in the last chapter, if you believe that it's your responsibility to smooth out all conflicts and make every relationship peaceful, and an Emotional Predator is relentlessly fighting with you, then you're likely to feel guilty, burdened and failed. A kind-hearted, generous woman spent decades absorbing abuse in her marriage because she believed that it was her job to make conflicts go away, and standing up to the abuse felt like adding to the conflict. Eventually this drove her to the brink of suicide before she realized that putting up with abuse wasn't her job in life but *a role she had accepted in a story written by others,* and that putting up with abuse didn't reduce conflict, it prolonged it. She wrote a new story for herself and divorced her Emotional Predator.

If one of your core values is to help everyone, and an Emotional Predator is taking everything you give and demanding more, then you're likely to feel frustrated and inadequate. But on the other hand, if you believe that his insatiable demands aren't your creation or responsibility, then you're not likely to blame yourself for them. And if your core value is to help *only* those who help themselves and take responsibility for themselves, then you're not likely to feel frustrated or inadequate when he blames you for not doing enough for him. You won't waste your energy on him.

Although many stories can create emotional vulnerabilities that Emotional Predators exploit, stories that assign blame are particularly dangerous. An Emotional Predator will blame you to induce guilt, and then use your guilt to blackmail and control you. Guilt is blaming yourself, and blaming yourself plays into his hands by agreeing with him that you're the cause of problems. The remedy isn't to *shift* blame onto him and enter a battle over which of you is "really" to blame. The remedy is to *transcend* stories involving blame (and thus guilt) altogether.

Blame and guilt are *options* that you should pass up. Blame (of yourself or another person) is a story that creates a moral melodrama that adds nothing productive to an already disorienting situation. It's enough to know that an Emotional Predator, like a large wild carnivore, is dangerous. We don't *blame* a lion for being a lion, but we take precautions around lions. Even if we think Emotional Predators are profoundly wicked and depraved (i.e. evil), we don't need to add a moral element to protect ourselves and our loved ones. Adding a moral element of blame injects emotion which inhibits our ability to protect.

When we assign blame, we pick one "cause" out of a series of events going back into the distant past. Any cause we pick is arbitrary because it inevitably will have been preceded by prior causes. Couples fighting routinely enter this "chicken and egg" debate when they assign blame to the other person in the guise of trying to figure out what's cause and what's effect. The husband might say "the problem is you never initiate sex." The wife might respond with "you never appreciate anything I do, so I don't feel like sex." The husband might reply "Well you don't appreciate all my sacrifices, so I don't see why I should feel appreciative of you." And so on. Traditional theories of psychology play into this when they assign cause (i.e. blame) to our parents. But if our parents "caused" our problems, then the true cause must be what their parents and their parents' parents did, on back into the unknowable past.

So stories about our relationships that level blame are really fictions that pick an arbitrary cause out of an unbroken series of events. Situations are complex and evolving. Re-writing your interpersonal stories so that they don't assign cause is a good way to gain control over your life by liberating you from the manipulations of blame and guilt. I'm not saying you shouldn't take *responsibility* for the consequences of your choices. But taking responsibility for your choices, and not letting an Emotional Predator skirt responsibility for hers, isn't the same as blaming. If you want clarity and freedom from manipulation, leave melodramatic moralizing blame out of it.

Assuming that all people are basically like you is another dangerous story. Kind-hearted and generous souls who live this myth give indiscriminately in the mistaken belief and hope that "of course" everyone will give back. But when he gives to an Emotional Predator, a generous soul finds himself repeatedly used and abandoned. Waiting in vain for reciprocal generosity, appreciation and kindness from an Emotional Predator is a fool's errand.

A good man I know lived two hours from his Emotional Predator sister. He did all of the traveling to see her, always seeing her at her apartment. The only time she traveled to him was when a famous musician she loved was playing in his town, which made the trip worthwhile to her. But she'd complain that he didn't do enough, wasn't trying hard enough, wasn't there for her in their relationship. It took an act of extreme selfishness from her, but he finally saw who she was, rejected her one-sided taking and blame, and limited his contact.

Changing your beliefs and stories about yourself and others isn't as radical as it may sound. Decades ago when I practiced law, I gave a friend of mine thousands of dollars of free legal work. For over a year while I was helping him with his legal problem, this friend and I saw each other weekly and spoke on the phone almost daily. As soon as I transferred his file to another lawyer and he no longer needed my help, my friend stopped returning my calls and disappeared. For about a year I felt betrayed by him, until I realized that *I had betrayed myself* by assuming that he shared my belief about what a friend is.

To me, a friend is someone whose back you have, someone you're there for when they need you, someone you do everything you can for. I absorbed that story from my father without realizing it, believing it was universally true for everyone. But to this vanished "friend," a friend is someone who's useful to him. In his world, once I stopped being useful to him, I was no longer his friend. *I had created my own one-way-street relationship problem by naively assuming that he (and everyone else) shared my story about what a friend is.* Changing my story to accept that what others mean by "friend" is not necessarily the same as what I mean by "friend" has allowed me to see the more mercenary stories some people have about friendship. I didn't change my definition of a friend. I changed my naive story that everyone else shared my definition and I accepted a wider range of what other people are capable of. This was part of my learning that other people aren't necessarily like me in important ways, which has protected me from one-way street relationships.

For purposes of protecting yourself, you are what you believe, in the sense that your core values, beliefs and assumptions about yourself in a world of others - your stories - determine what information you take in, how you interpret events and others, how you feel, and how you react and respond. Your stories about yourself mold your experience and emotions, and can expose or protect you. You've written them from templates provided by both the larger culture and the micro-cultures of family and peers.

Much more than we would like to admit, our memory and perception are *selective, creative acts*. We see what we want to see and hear what we want to hear. We also do *not* see what we do *not* want to see and do *not* hear what we do *not* want to hear. Delusion is near universal and almost always a mistake. Extremely intelligent people delude themselves all the time, enlisting their intelligence to justify underlying assumptions that are arbitrary. The more you're locked into your stories about who you are or who you must be, the less you're able to see clearly, take evasive measures and repel Emotional Predators. So it's helpful to loosen your grip on what you think you know and re-consider what you take to be unassailable truth. To that end, consider where your beliefs originated, and how they originated in choices you didn't know you were making.

SOURCES OF OUR STORIES

The stories we tell ourselves are creations of the cultures of country, region, ethnicity, religion, economic class, family, and politics that we grew up with and live in. These stories aren't inherent in the human condition. For example, although death is universal to all people, the stories humans have told about death are many and varied. My story about what a friend is, that I'd assumed was shared by everyone, came to me from my father. Change your stories and you change your emotions.[27] Changing your stories about yourself in relationship can change feeling trapped, suffocated and vulnerable, to feeling free, liberated and untouchable.

Our memories are a central part of our stories. They form the basis of our identity, telling us who we are and who we want to be. We like to think our memory is like a file cabinet that holds unchanging material that we pull out whenever we want. Then when we're done, that material automatically goes back into the file where we can find it unchanged later on. Or to use the more contemporary metaphor, we think memory is like a computer hard drive with files that we can open unchanged from the way they were when they were saved. We think of memory problems as difficulty opening the folder or file we want.

But research shows that our memories are much more pliable than that and problems of memory are much more subtle. Suggestions from others can lead us to construct false memories and delusions. And, again, delusion is almost always a mistake. Psychologist Elizabeth Loftus has shown how suggestions can plant false memories and pointed out that repercussions of false memory can be positive or negative. She speculates that future "mind technology" might allow us to use suggestions to implant designer memories to enhance our identity. For our purposes, it's enough to realize that Emotional Predators use suggestion to distort our memories in a negative direction, degrading our sense of self to serve their own ends. With practice and independent fact checking, you can take control of your memory processes and use them to build a stronger sense of self.

Even without suggestions from others, all on our own we distort our memories to either enhance or diminish our self-esteem. You may know someone who sincerely exaggerates their failures or successes and thinks they're being accurate. Dr. Steve Ramirez, a neuroscientist, has conducted experiments to edit or erase memories with lasers targeted in the hippocampus area of the brain. He concluded that "we reinvent ourselves daily with the new memories that we form." Dr. Ramirez believes that the same part of the brain that recalls memory, including false memories, is also the part that lets us imagine ourselves in future scenarios. It allows us to choose to be reactive or flexible about our future. He speculates that the laser technology he uses (he calls it "optogenetics") may be able to suppress the emotional component of a memory and leave the facts intact. Again, for our purposes, it's enough to realize that (through meditation and other techniques) you can detach emotion from memory and fact, and choose between stories that foster dangerous reactivity and ones that foster protective strategy.

Experiments done in the 1970s demonstrated that we perceive and believe the data that supports the beliefs we already hold, and ignore and discount data that challenge our pre-existing beliefs. This is called confirmation bias. Other studies have shown that (by definition) we don't know what we don't know, and *when we're ignorant, we believe we know more than we do.* At least in the United States incompetent people regularly over-estimate their competence, creating illusory feelings of superiority.[28] In Asian cultures, people may under-estimate their competence. Either way, *when we don't know, the real difficulty is that we don't know that we don't know.* All of this suggests that we would do well to loosen our grip on what we think we know.

We can never know everything about our self or someone else with complete accuracy. Our information about anyone has three parts: what's more or less accurately known (the known), what's made up stories (the BS), and what's not fully or accurately known (the mysterious). To calm our fear of the unknown we fill in what's mysterious with BS stories we make up. Paradoxically, the more comfortable you are with not-knowing, the less you need to make up delusional stories - thus the more accurately you know. And stories about who you must be in order to be a good person can be among the most dangerous, leading you into co-dependent and vulnerable relationships with Emotional Predators. It turns out that not-knowing is the way to know more.

Knowing more (and more accurately) than an Emotional Predator knows - about yourself, the Emotional Predator and the situation - is essential. So embrace the paradox that, to gain more accurate knowledge you need to remain skeptical about what you think you know. Realize that your stories are adopted, not intrinsic, parts of you - as much fiction as fact. When you open yourself to learning new things, when you see how the stories you've inhabited make you vulnerable, it becomes easier to muster the courage to consider new perspectives and change. And the only thing you can change is yourself. "[T]he accomplishment of true insight is indissolubly connected with a change in character."[29] So enjoy exploring new stories - other options for life. And don't beat yourself up over your old self-defeating stories.

ALTERNATIVES TO A FEW COMMON STORIES

As you look at the stories you live by - the core beliefs and values you hold, and the memories you return to - consider alternative stories that might protect you better. The story that we are one "self" is the first one to let go of. We like to think of ourselves as one person, but actually we have many different aspects; we're different in different situations and with different people. A wise person can be blunt in one situation and diplomatic in another, generous in one and stingy in another.

Embracing your different "situational" selves lets you bring forth different responses to meet the needs of different situations. The wider your range of options for responding, the safer you are. To meet the challenges of an Emotional Predator, it's useful to bring forward whatever aspect of yourself is the most strategically wise in each situation. To do that, you need to be open to a variety of stories about yourself and others. Let's look at a few alternatives to some common stories that make us vulnerable (some we've already touched on in Chapter 4 about *Self-victimizing Beliefs*), and how those alternatives can protect us.

One variant of a story that assigns blame is the meritocracy myth: the common belief that good things happen to good people who work hard - which brings with it the unspoken corollary that bad things must happen to bad people who are lazy. If you live this story and you're suffering abuse from an Emotional Predator, the abuse - the bad thing happening to you - will be "proof" of your moral failing and you'll blame yourself. Sounds wacky, but it's amazing how many people blame themselves for being abused. They live out this meritocracy myth story without noticing that it's fiction and that they can choose to believe something else.

A more useful and accurate alternative to the meritocracy myth is acceptance of randomness. If you're being abused by an Emotional Predator, a bad thing is in fact happening to you, but that doesn't mean you're bad, defective or lazy. Bizarre as it may sound, the opposite may be true. Because Emotional Predators target people with strong consciences that can be manipulated by guilt and shame, being targeted by an Emotional Predator may indicate you're a particularly *good* person. You were just in the wrong place at the wrong time and fell into her clutches without recognizing the danger. Your generosity, empathy and good conscience probably attracted her.

Similar to the meritocracy myth, many of us believe that to be a good person we need to take care of others, but in doing so we confuse taking care of someone with *enabling and co-dependent caretaking*. Taking care of someone isn't taking responsibility for the other person's choices and feelings. Good people are in danger when they try to help someone who isn't taking responsibility for himself and first doing all he can to help himself. That kind of dangerous co-dependent helping is a form of addiction that serves neither person.

Decent, generous, hardworking, sensitive, kind and gifted people give of themselves to others. They do this naturally and without thinking twice or even noticing they're doing it. But when they also habitually ask for little or nothing in return, they're at risk (and not as helpful as they think). Emotional Predators seek out those people and take, take, take from them, giving little or nothing back. When an Emotional Predator has taken all he can get (when he has drained the good person dry), or when he sees someone else from whom he thinks he can take more, he leaves. And he often leaves with the projected accusation that the generous person was "selfish." So, *people who believe that it's good and right to always give without tracking what comes back can find themselves repeatedly used, drained and abandoned.* These generous souls give in the belief that the other will reciprocate. They wrongly assume that the other person is basically like them. None of that makes them bad people.

Being a good person doesn't mean being a sucker. Altruism toward an Emotional Predator isn't useful and can be dangerous. Enabling them makes them worse, and good people can fall into an *empathy trap* where they shower Emotional Predators with empathy and generosity only to be taken advantage of. With Emotional Predators, it's usually the case that *no good deed goes unpunished.* So be selective about who you bestow your good deeds upon. Reject the story that good people are altruistic toward everyone.

Do you have relationships where you give and sacrifice, and you get used and discarded - where you're there for the other person when they need you, but the other person isn't there for you when you need them? In an odd way, both people in these relationships share the same mission: you're there for the other person, and the other person also is there for the other person. In these relationships, both of you are there for the same person: the person who is *not* you. Emotional Predators set up their relationships that way.

To guard against this kind of destructive co-dependent care-taking, monitor how your needs are or are not being respected and met in your relationships. Assess your relationships for one-way streets, paying attention to the flows of energy, money, time and emotional support. If a relationship is a one-way street, with most or all of the value and effort flowing from you to the other person, but little or none returning, then change things. Either get off that street, or if you can't exit, then implement strategies that will re-balance the flow and stop the drain from you. That requires alternative stories about what it means to be a good person.

One alternative story to co-dependent care-taking is that *a good person only helps folks who've done all they can to help themselves and who take full responsibility for their own choices*. Those people truly merit help and helping them isn't enabling their bad choices. And this alternative story also says that a good person doesn't help folks who are lazy or irresponsible. With those folks, a good person lets the consequences of their choices fall on them. Sometimes that helps lazy or irresponsible folks take responsibility for themselves. Sometimes not. With an Emotional Predator, letting the consequences of his choices fall on him keeps you from being abused and manipulated.

The common belief that we cause other people to feel the emotions they feel is another myth that makes us vulnerable. This is embedded in our language when people say "You make me feel ...". In fact, you never "make" anyone feel anything emotionally. *People's emotions are generated by the beliefs they have about themselves and others*. The way each of us interprets and reacts to stimuli is different depending on what each of us learned growing up and the stories we adopted to adapt. Subjected to the same scolding tirade, one person will cry because they believe that being scolded means they've done something wrong, but another will laugh because they believe they've done nothing wrong and people who scold are just displaying their own problems.

Emotional Predators use our common mistaken belief that we cause other people's feelings as a powerful lever to get what they want from us. An Emotional Predator may try to use guilt by convincing you that you're the cause of her unhappiness. Or she may try to use flattery by convincing you that you're the cause of her great joy and happiness. Don't buy into either of these. Don't take responsibility for other people's feelings, even though that can feel seductively potent. *Take responsibility for your actions and words, not how someone chooses to interpret them.* Reject the story that you are "causing" an Emotional Predator to feel or experience anything.

If an Emotional Predator has used one of your self-victimizing stories to manipulate you, it doesn't mean there's something wrong with you. As we've seen, Emotional Predators target good people to take advantage of their generosity and ample consciences. So being targeted by an Emotional Predator can be a kind of bizarre compliment and confirmation that there's something very *right* with you. Choose that alternative to the meritocracy story that bad things don't happen to good people.

Don't be afraid to change yourself. You can always go back to your old stories, assumptions, beliefs and habits. When you're open to changing yourself, new possibilities arise. When you let go of limiting beliefs and stories, you free up tremendous amounts of energy and vitality, and your vision clears and your options expand. These are all extremely useful when dealing with an Emotional Predator.

SELF-CARE: POSITIVE PRACTICES TO BOOST YOUR MORALE AND BUILD FORTITUDE

When you're dealing with an Emotional Predator, don't forget to take care of yourself and find things that keep your morale up. You are your most valuable tool. To keep yourself in good repair, remember to have fun, relax and feel good. As you focus on protection, remember to nurture yourself and practice self-care. It builds inner resources you need.

Self-care is like re-charging your inner battery after life has drained it. And there's no greater drain than an Emotional Predator. What other things drain you? What recharges you? For example, some people tend to feel refreshed from time alone and others tend to feel refreshed from time with others. Anything that relaxes and calms you, anything that feeds your soul and brings you joy, will boost your morale.

The options for nurturing yourself are almost limitless and include many of the ways to know yourself better mentioned in Chapter 4. Meditating and being still, being physically activity and exercising, eating well, getting massages, practicing yoga, hiking, walking, running, dancing, having social contact with safe groups, setting aside alone time (perhaps with electronic devices turned off), creating and appreciating art and music, being in nature, sensory deprivation, traveling, gardening, cooking, spending time with animals, reading, psychedelics, guided imagery are a few things I have seen people use to clear their mind, relax and replenish their inner resources. The possibilities are almost endless.

When in doubt, try something with an open mind. I know people for whom weight lifting is a calming meditative practice. For others, it's painting in an art studio. For others, it's repairing old cars and solving mechanical problems in the garage or house. For others, it's giving the house a good cleaning, painting a room a new color or cooking. To be restorative, the activity just has to focus your mind on something calming while excluding all the other mental chatter and noise that normally bombards us. Detailed exploration of ways to care for yourself is beyond the scope of this book, but let's take a quick look at a few that I've seen be particularly useful to people dealing with an Emotional Predator.

Nourishing Positive Relationships and Support Systems

Cultivating positive, nourishing relationships, and building support systems and emotional safe harbors, are potent ways to improve your morale. Contact with *screened and selected* folks outside the Emotional Predator's universe expands your reserves of courage and affirms your experience and perspective. Even when you feel tired and drained, it can be worthwhile to rally enough to get out and connect with trusted friends and loved ones, if only for a short visit. In person is best, but the phone or an internet video chat can do you a world of good.

The isolation a target feels from being "gaslighted" is a big part of the trauma wrought by an Emotional Predator, so don't let yourself be cut off from safe, independent support that can help you reclaim your reality. Check things out with safe folks who were around when the Emotional Predator did (or did not do) something or before you met him. Get outside opinions from trustworthy friends and relatives, folks with lots of good old-fashioned common sense and time to hear you out. But don't be disappointed if your neighbors or friends can't stick with you when you revisit all the details of your experience with the Emotional Predator.

But also beware of "yes" friends who'll reinforce your old unhelpful stories. You need to *challenge* your old stories, beliefs and assumptions. Your true friends may be those who're willing to risk telling you things that they fear you might not want to hear. How many times have you seen friends wait until *after* the breakup to tell someone how they never liked the ex? If you're dealing with an Emotional Predator, you need friends who'll risk telling you now how they really feel. Give your true friends permission to tell you what they really think of a problem person in your life, and when you hear negative things from several trusted people, take them seriously. Consider joining a therapy group of high functioning people run by a therapist who truly understands Emotional Predators and carefully screens them out of the group.

Humor and Gratitude

In all things, and particularly in dealing with Emotional Predators, it's very helpful to find and maintain your sense of humor. Humor is priceless, free and easily overlooked. Easier said than done when you're in dark times, but *finding humor in all things widens your perspective and immunizes you in powerful ways.* In almost every case, you can *choose* whether to laugh or cry at the outlandish things an Emotional Predator does. Choosing to see humor in yourself and your situation relieves the stress that Emotional Predators prey on.

Cultivating your sense of humor is as important as anything else you do. Humor has been defined as *benign* transgressions - favorably going beyond limits - and favorably going beyond limits is one way to describe the change in your beliefs that can be so protective. Humor connects you to your humanity and strengthens your humility, both important for staying grounded and connected to reality. And when you're more humble, it's easier to loosen your grip on the stories you live by and try alternatives. Finding ways to laugh about yourself and others, including the Emotional Predator (but not in front of him), is a great way to expand your options, relieve stress and calm yourself.

Even the most frightening Emotional Predator can be brought down to size and made less scary by the judicious application of a little humor. If you can't imagine that, watch Charlie Chaplin making fun of Adolph Hitler in the 1940 film, *The Great Dictator*. Winston Churchill is reputed to have said that he calmed his nerves before meeting with Joseph Stalin by imagining him on the toilet. But don't ridicule or make fun of an Emotional Predator to his face.

Dealing with an Emotional Predator can feel like a deep tragedy. But *tragedy and comedy are the same thing viewed from opposite perspectives.* As Joni Mitchell put it, "Laughing and crying, you know it's the same release." So make every effort to find the humor in what may feel tragic. *Laughter is one of the greatest, and most easily overlooked, antidotes to toxic adversities in life.* No matter how grim things seem, there are always opportunities to laugh. Today YouTube offers an endless supply of funny clips, from classic comedians of the past to current talk show silliness. Time spent watching clips that make you laugh is time well spent.[30] When you're laughing, you can't feel fearful, anxious, doubting, depressed or other uncomfortable emotions that Emotional Predators prey on.

Closely aligned to opportunities to laugh, there are always opportunities to feel *grateful*. Practicing gratitude is useful in every aspect of living. David Stendl-Rast described this well in a TED talk that's worth listening to. To summarize, in each moment there are many things to be grateful for. That's not to say that we should be grateful for everything. There are certainly plenty of things that aren't so great and for which we aren't grateful. But in every moment there also are plenty of things, often very simple things, that we can *choose* to be grateful for. In each moment that we choose gratitude, there's no room for negative emotions or thoughts. Try it. Pick something in your life that you can be grateful for and let yourself feel gratitude for it. Notice how, as long as you are feeling gratitude, the gratitude pushes out all negative feelings and brings calm.

Each moment offers you many opportunities to laugh and feel grateful. And if you miss the opportunity in one moment, the next moment offers it again. So seek out laughter and gratitude even in the darkest hours. Choose to laugh and be grateful.

Taking the Long View and Playing

Another useful practice is to take a long view of things. Recognize that over time what initially appears to be disaster can turn out to be good fortune, and vice versa. Taking a long view helps us relax and de-stress over events whose ultimate outcome isn't known to us. An ancient Chinese text[31] makes this point with the parable of a poor farmer whose horse ran off into the country of the barbarians. The farmer's neighbors offered their condolences, but his father asked, "How do you know that this isn't *good* fortune?". After some time, the horse returned with an excellent barbarian horse. His neighbors offered their congratulations, but his father asked, "How do you know that this isn't a disaster?". The two horses bred, and the family became rich with many fine horses. The farmer's son rode and trained them. One day he fell off and broke his hip, leaving him crippled. The farmer's neighbors offered him their condolences, but his father asked "How do you know that this isn't good fortune?". A year later, war broke out and all the able-bodied young men were conscripted. Nine-tenths of them died in the war. Thus, good fortune can be disaster, and disaster can be good fortune. We can't know how events will be transformed. So loosen your grip on the way you interpret events. What seems today like a disaster imposed by an Emotional Predator may be the beginning of the unraveling of her power. Time will tell. Loosening your grip on your beliefs about disaster and good fortune in this way - taking a long view - makes you less emotionally reactive.

Here's how a former client described his experience with taking a long term view and gratitude: "My career goal was to become the CTO of a company and now I've made it; but, interestingly it wasn't because of some master plan I had. Failure (losing my job at my old company) turned into an opportunity that would never have happened without the failure. So, one never knows what good will arise out of something that seems so bad at the time. It's a bit humbling and ironic to have the lack of control cause the success that my efforts to control things failed to achieve. ;-) I feel very fortunate."

Another way to lighten up and loosen your grip on self-victimizing beliefs is to *draw no sharp distinction between your work and play, your labor and leisure, your mind and body, your education and recreation*. Instead, just pursue excellence through whatever you do and leave others to label what you're doing. Play at your work and work at your play. Combine your labor and leisure, your mind and body, and your education and recreation.

Drawing no distinction between your work and play, your labor and leisure, is related to the Buddhist insight that suffering arises from seeking to prolong pleasure and avoid pain. Pursuing excellence in whatever you do offers an alternative to being caught in a web of attraction to what you want and aversion from what you don't want. The late Zen teacher John Daido Loori, Roshi, told me that things we seek and things we avoid are merely creations of our mind - which for our purposes means creations of our core beliefs and operative stories.

Find things that improve your morale, build fortitude and raise your self-esteem - all without deprecating self-judgment and dumping on yourself. Don't "should" on yourself. Choose to be a confident, self-aware person that Emotional Predators will avoid.

chapter six

Step 4 - How to Disengage and Avoid an Emotional Predator

It's always better to avoid danger and harm when possible.

"You are under the unfortunate delusion that simply because you run away from danger, you have no courage. You're confusing courage with wisdom."
Oz, First Wizard Deluxe

"Run, you fools!"
Gandolf, the Grey Wizard

DO NOT ENGAGE, DO NOT CONFRONT

The wizards are right. Have the wisdom to run from Emotional Predators whenever you can. When you identify an Emotional Predator in your world, *the best thing to do is avoid engaging* with them. That's easiest when she isn't targeting you and you're observing her from the sidelines. In that situation, just steer clear and avoid involvement. This should be done politely and without any hint that you see anything wrong or negative about her. You certainly shouldn't explain to an Emotional Predator the real reason you're moving away. If she asks, some version of the old line from dating of "It's not you, it's me" is usually the best approach. Be too busy. Make vague circumstances the "bad cop" that forces you to decline engaging with her.

As you move away from an Emotional Predator, *don't explain or justify*, just state your unavailability in the briefest way possible. "I have too much going on," without being drawn into listing and justifying what else you have going on, is usually enough. Particularly after you've already said you aren't available, often the most powerful response to further inquiry is no response at all. Silence can speak loudly and clearly (and uses the Emotional Predator tactic of passive-aggression for protection). Be as invisible as you can, showing neither fear nor vulnerability, joy nor excitement, satisfaction nor disappointment. Show no emotion at all, because your emotions are what an Emotional Predator feeds on and will try to manipulate.

If you find yourself already engaged with an Emotional Predator, the best thing to do is disengage. But that may not always be possible. If the Emotional Predator is in your family or at your work, you may need to, or you may choose to, stay engaged. Chapter 7 describes tactics for protecting yourself when you're staying engaged. The rest of this Chapter 6 describes some of those tactics that are particularly useful for disengaging. As we'll see, *strategically disengaging is itself a special type of temporary engagement with the goal of permanently disengaging*. So we'll introduce tactics here for disengaging and revisit them in more detail in Chapter 7.

Not every tactic is helpful in every situation. Tactics are tools and it's best to have a full toolbox even if you don't need some tools for every job. You have to use judgment about which tools to use in a particular situation or with a particular Emotional Predator. And sometimes you can't know how effective a tactic could be until you try it.

In communicating with an Emotional Predator, almost always *less is more*. An Emotional Predator will lure you into divulging too much information - by pretending to be ignorant and innocent, or by feigning great interest, or by challenging you to justify yourself - and then use that information to manipulate you. Emotional Predators understand much more than they let on and part of their manipulation is getting you to reveal and expose yourself. Resist the natural instinct to explain or educate. In particular, resist the urge to be deeply known by someone you don't know well. Resist the urge to explain or show Emotional Predators three things you want them to see clearly: you, them, and reality. Instead of explaining or showing what you know, *know it, don't show it.* As Skipper the Penguin from the movie *Madagascar* instructs his crew, "Just smile and wave, boys. Smile and wave."

When you're dealing with an Emotional Predator, it pays to hold your cards close. Control the information she has about you and what you know. Don't thoughtlessly reveal who you are, what you observe or (most importantly) what you care about. She'll use information about you to manipulate you. She'll use the information about how you see her to improve her facade and hide better. (Exposing an Emotional Predator *to third parties* is different and will be discussed in Chapter 7.) She'll use your view of reality to craft ways to mess with you through gaslighting and other manipulations. So disclosures to an Emotional Predator should always be for a sound strategic reason, never for your emotional release or gratification, or in pursuit of unattainable goals.

Consider carefully before confronting or trying to expose an Emotional Predator to herself. Confronting her obviously brings you into her sights and it rarely changes her behaviors (and won't change her nature), unless enough negative *public exposure* is involved. And beware. An exposed Emotional Predator will have a long memory and may seek revenge when the opportunity arises, sometimes long after you've forgotten and moved on. As President, Barak Obama notoriously ridiculed then citizen Donald Trump at a televised public correspondent's dinner. Some believe getting revenge for this public humiliation helped motivate President Trump's 2016 campaign and that after his election, he enacted his revenge by relentlessly undoing many of Obama's Executive Orders and policies. Whether you love or hate these politicians, it remains true that confronting an Emotional Predator invites her attack, always a risky thing to do.

Your instinct and desire to help others is part of what makes you a good person. But *helping others can get you into trouble when an Emotional Predator is involved.* As you've read this book, a number of people you know may have come to mind as possible Emotional Predators or their targets. You may want to help someone you see being abused and manipulated, and think you should expose the Emotional Predator to their target or third parties or, more dangerously, confront the Emotional Predator. Wanting to help is a noble impulse that confirms your decency and humanity, but don't underestimate the risk to yourself.

For an Emotional Predator you're either with them or against them. Once he notices you through your efforts to help his target, he'll regard you as his enemy. Confronting or intervening with him invites attack. And unless you're very careful, even if you don't confront him directly, trying to expose him to others also can bring you into his sights. Once you share things (with his target or someone else), it's not possible to control where that information goes.

Trying to educate his target is less risky than confronting the Emotional Predator. But be cautious. If your friend is falling under his spell, she may refuse to accept anything you tell her, and she may even align with him against you. More than once, I've seen a good person try to expose an Emotional Predator to his target, only to have the target share the helper's observations with the Emotional Predator. The target may be too weak or disturbed herself to act prudently, or she may naively think that telling the Emotional Predator what you said about him will somehow change him. Sometimes all you can do is accept that people see what they want to see, suggest readings[32] and leave them to their fate.

So when you see an Emotional Predator with whom who you're not already engaged (or when you want to disengage from one), the best way to protect yourself is to get away and resist your impulse to expose or confront the Emotional Predator. The next sections look at the vital importance of being unprovoked - when disengaging or in any other interactions with an Emotional Predator.

IF YOU'RE ALREADY ENGAGED, THEN DISENGAGE - DO NOT BE PROVOKED

The best situation is to spot an Emotional Predator before you've engaged in any interactions and then steer clear. More often, you spot an Emotional Predator only after you've become involved. There's no shame in that. It can take repeated interactions to alert us to the patterns that signal we're dealing with an Emotional Predator. When you do notice you've gotten involved with one that you didn't spot early enough to completely avoid, the next best thing is to disengage - withdraw from the field of battle, so to speak - and leave her to look elsewhere for someone to dominate and abuse. Don't underestimate the wisdom of cutting your losses by disengaging.

Disengaging should be done strategically, not impulsively. When dealing with an Emotional Predator, it's always wise to pick your battles. You may feel outraged or betrayed and want to assert yourself in the situation or to the Emotional Predator. That's almost always a fool's errand. Never take the bait and react emotionally or be provoked or drawn into a debate or discussion. That would just drain you and reveal tactical and emotional information. As they say, arguing with a crazy person is crazy. If you can avoid all future battles by walking away, don't think twice, walk away.

As in all dealings with an Emotional Predator, when disengaging conceal your true emotions, particularly your emotional reactions to her. That means *playing an Emotional Predator's game of managing appearances better than she does.* Even if you *feel* yourself internally provoked, let her think you're immune and indifferent.

When you prevent an Emotional Predator from reading your emotions, you disarm many of her core weapons and you starve her motivation for targeting you. Use her tactic of provoking you against her, provoking *her* by remaining an unprovoked emotional blank screen. Showing no emotional reactions has three defensive benefits: 1) it *removes the Emotional Predator's motivation* for targeting you; 2) it *makes her true nature visible* to you and others, removing her weapon of stealth; and 3) by hiding your personal emotional world, it *denies her ammunition* she needs to attack you.

Because Emotional Predators feed their craving for power, control and domination with your emotional reactions, keeping those reactions unseen removes much of an Emotional Predator's motivation. Getting you to react emotionally gratifies their need to be the "puppet-master." They love watching you jump when they say "Boo!" or run around in circles chasing impossible, crazy and wasteful irrelevancies, or struggle to explain obvious things they pretend not to understand. When you allow yourself to be provoked, the Emotional Predator feels powerful simply from inducing some internal reaction in you. When you allow yourself to be shuttled into his agendas, he feels powerful from getting you to jump through his hoops. But when you deny him the gratification of seeing his provocations succeed, he eventually gets bored and seeks that gratification from another target.

If you remain unprovoked and don't get upset (or at least don't show it), the Emotional Predator is likely at first to ramp up his provocations. He's involved with you to get you to react emotionally so he can feel powerful. (He's not there because of whatever flattering praise he's heaped on you. It's not about you. It's all about him.) When you remain unprovoked, showing bland even bored responses, be ready for more urgent attempts to provoke you. If you anticipate these increased provocations, you'll be better able to resist being drawn into reacting or showing emotion. Stay the course, don't gratify his need to feel powerful. Frustrate that motivation for targeting you and he'll eventually seek easier prey elsewhere.

The second benefit of not being provoked to show emotions is it makes the Emotional Predator more visible. If you don't react, she can't distract attention from her poor behavior by pointing to your reaction. *And not being provoked yourself provokes the Emotional*

Predator to show her true nature as she increases her provocations. When she ramps up her provocations, those poor behaviors are easier to see. I've seen many slick "easy-going" Emotional Predators become curt, sarcastic, snide and bitchy as they grew more frustrated when their targets didn't react to their provocations. Public exposure disarms an Emotional Predator's weapon of stealth and, because she's driven to maintain a positive public facade, it pressures her to move on. Seeing her more clearly also helps you stand firm.

The third benefit of not being provoked to show emotions is it denies the Emotional Predator information that he would use as ammunition against you. As we've seen, the things you hold nearest and dearest to your heart - your core beliefs and values - are the things an Emotional Predator uses to manipulate you. The less he knows about these things, the better. When you expose your emotional reactions, you provide him with ammunition which he'll enjoy using against you. An exasperated "stop blaming me," tells him that you're vulnerable to feeling blamed. On the other hand, when you deny him information about your emotions, he eventually runs low on ammunition and looks for a more compliant target. So don't be provoked into revealing your emotional states (or tactical information in a draining debate).

Remember that an Emotional Predator's provocations will be skillfully targeted at your unique, personal emotional vulnerabilities, so it can be tougher than you think to remain perfectly unprovoked. Be kind and patient with yourself if you notice he got under your skin. If you miss the opportunity to remain unprovoked in one moment, the next moment always offers you another opportunity. And if it's not possible to be calm and unprovoked internally, and you still feel triggered, then at least seize the always available opportunity to restore your blank screen that hides your emotional reactions. Later in this chapter we'll look at three levels of being unprovoked.

PROJECTIVE IDENTIFICATION: A POWERFUL KIND OF PROVOCATION

Closely related to gratifying an Emotional Predator's need to dominate, letting her provoke emotional reactions from you also serves her *psychological need to relieve her inner discomfort* through a subtle process called projective identification. Projective identification is a process where one person who is emotionally disturbed *transfers* their own inner turmoil to someone else. Using projective identification, Emotional Predators *unburden themselves of uncomfortable feelings by provoking those feelings in you* - feelings that aren't native to you. They transfer their inner disturbance to you, using your empathy as a receiver. Without knowing they're doing it, it's as though they're saying "I can't handle these bad feelings ... Here, you take them," and they hand them over to you.

Projective identification is related to *projection*, an Ego defense described by Anna Freud and now commonly understood. With both projection and projective identification, a disturbed person doesn't have enough inner strength to grow up and face her disturbing feelings. So those feelings remain stuck in her psyche, an irritant just out of awareness. In projection, she copes by blocking them out of her own awareness and instead *seeing* them "out there" in others (or the world).

A person projecting is like a movie projector (hence the term projection), seeing her own uncomfortable feelings in another - feelings that aren't innately part of the other person. Projection isn't done intentionally. A person projecting doesn't know she's doing it, although she sometimes can recognize her projections later, usually with help from a good therapist. When someone's projecting onto you, it feels strangely like she's talking about someone else not you, because the things she's saying about you aren't how others see you or how you see yourself. An angry person projecting her anger onto you will tell you how angry *you* are when you're actually calm and peaceful. Projection is used by most of us from time to time. *Projective identification*, however, is used by more seriously disturbed people.

Projective identification is like super charged projection. In projective identification, the person disowning her own negative experience not only *sees* those feelings in someone else, she *actively provokes* them in the other person by mistreating him, often through passive aggression.

An angry wife who can't face her own anger will pretend to herself and the world that she's calm and peaceful, while she sees her husband as angry. That's projection. But when projective identification is active, she'll also withhold all kinds of things and do all kinds of nasty things to provoke an angry reaction from him. When he takes the bait and becomes angry, the wife is "confirmed" in her delusion that people around her are angry, not her - and it looks to all the world like he has an anger problem. But properly understood, the husband's anger isn't really *his* anger. It's *the wife's* anger that she's *transferred* to him by provoking him. His empathy, his capacity to feel what others feel, is the medium that carries her anger to him.

Projective identification is closely related to the experience that psychoanalysts call *transference*. Transference can be seen as a form of projective identification that happens in the analyst-patient relationship. In psychoanalytic transference, without knowing he's doing it, the patient will subtly provoke in the analyst experiences and feelings the patient can't tolerate in himself. An analyst who sees 20 patients each week finds that one patient continually rejects the analyst's interpretations, telling the analyst that she isn't helping. This patient's parents always belittled and denigrated him, and the patient's core struggle is against feeling incompetent and worthless. Because of the patient's repeated rejections and criticisms, with this patient the analyst starts to feel that she's incompetent and worthless. But the analyst recognizes that she doesn't feel incompetent and worthless with any other patient, and she checks with a supervisor who confirms that her interventions with this patient are well thought out and insightful.

If this analyst realizes what's happening, she'll know that through transference, this patient is *inducing in the analyst* feelings that the patient suffers from and can't handle. The patient belittles and devalues the analyst in their sessions as his parents did to him during his childhood. The patient thus *transfers* to the analyst his own feelings of incompetence and worthlessness. Understood this way, the analyst can use the feelings of incompetence and worthlessness arising in her only with this patient as a window into feeling what it's like to be him. The analyst then separates those feelings from her own sense of self and uses them as education about the patient.

In your relations with an Emotional Predator, projective identification operates like psychoanalytic transference to shift his disowned negative experience into you. But that can only happen when you allow yourself to be emotionally provoked. Like the analyst, you can separate the Emotional Predator's inner world from your own.

Understanding projective identification helps you remain calm and keep an Emotional Predator's inner disturbance from polluting your inner world. If you find yourself accused of having an anger problem or other negative feelings, consider whether you felt similarly angry or negative *before* you met the person accusing you. If not, you may be the target of projective identification.

Understanding projective identification also provides you with a window to see into the Emotional Predator's inner disturbance. That deeper understanding of what goes on within him can help you counter his manipulations. But don't think you can use that information to change him into someone better. You can't.

When you don't take the bait and don't let yourself be provoked, you interrupt the projective identification process. The negative feelings the Emotional Predator is trying to unload on you stay put in him and he doesn't get the emotional pressure-relief of dumping them on you. Because he can't handle those feelings and he can't unload them on you, they begin to slip out through his false facade, making his true nature more visible. Others can see his disowned disturbing feelings (often anger) in *him* where they properly reside, rather than seeing them in you where he's transferred them by provoking you. Making the true nature of an Emotional Predator visible by rejecting projective identification can be a very powerful part of protecting yourself.

So whether you're disengaging from an Emotional Predator or restoring the balance of power if you remain engaged, do not accept projective identification. The defense to projective identification (and to many of the tactics of Emotional Predators) is to *refuse to allow yourself to be provoked.* That requires knowing your sensitive places and triggers.

The school yard saying "I know you are, but what am I? I'm rubber, you're glue. Everything you say bounces off me and sticks to you." is a nice way to deal with the projections and projective identification of an Emotional Predator. But say those things within yourself, not out loud to the other person. Katie was always regarded as funny, even-keeled and easy-going. Then she got involved with a slick Emotional Predator who denied that he was furious at his sexually abusive father. He repeatedly accused this easy-going woman of being angry, projecting his own anger onto her. He also used passive aggression and projective identification to provoke her. His relentless emotional abuse eventually escalated to physical violence. When he started shoving her around, she finally lost patience and shouted in fear and anger. Incredibly, he then claimed that her yelling to be left alone proved that *she* was the angry one. Fortunately, this stark reversal of truth helped Katie understand that his accusations were statements about himself. She saw them bouncing off her like she was rubber and sticking to him like he was glue, which gave her strength to calmly resist more provocations and extricate herself.

To summarize, through projective identification an Emotional Predator will reduce his inner tensions by unburdening himself of his disowned uncomfortable feelings and foisting them onto you, if you're willing to take them. He'll do this primarily through passive aggression, but also other provocations. When you let yourself be provoked, you end up carrying *his* anger, anxiety, fears, aggression, depression, or other negative feelings. But when you realize what's happening, those feelings become a window into the inner workings of his world. And when you stay unprovoked, his inner disturbance stays with him, making him more visible to others and keeping you free of that pollution.

So the benefits of being unprovoked include keeping your inner experience from being polluted, gaining better information about the Emotional Predator, keeping emotional information about you private, not gratifying his need to control and get reactions from you, and making him more visible - all of which disarms him and fortifies your defenses.

THREE LEVELS OF BEING UNPROVOKED

Looking more closely at resisting provocations, we see that there are three levels to being unprovoked. The first level is *not showing* any emotional reaction. That's a necessary start to protecting yourself whether you're disengaging or (as we'll see in the next chapter) staying involved. The second level, and better for protecting yourself, is to *not make any decisions* when you're having an emotional reaction. The third and most effective level of being unprovoked is to *have no emotional reaction at all.*

At that third and best level, you are nonplused, indifferent, even bored. Indifference is the strongest inner position to have. Indifference, not hate, is the opposite of love. To reach that level may take time. But you can get plenty of protection from the first two levels. At the first two levels, you may *feel* highly provoked, but you practice not showing that to the Emotional Predator and not making reactive decisions.

At all three levels of being unprovoked, the Emotional Predator doesn't see you having an emotional reaction to her provocations. This is a core aspect of controlling information. Even at the first level, when all you can manage is to not *show* your emotional reactions, be prepared for initial resistance and escalation from the Emotional Predator. In most cases, that'll be temporary and is a sign that your defenses are starting to work and that you're re-balancing the power in your favor. As we saw, when an Emotional Predator escalates, she becomes more visible, which is good for you. If you stay the course and remain boring and emotionally invisible to her, frustrating her need to elicit emotional reactions, she'll eventually move on.

One way to not show any reaction is to stick to the facts, only the relevant facts, and nothing but the relevant facts. To have facts ready, record and document things as they happen, but don't let the Emotional Predator know you're doing it. (In Chapter 7, we'll look into various ways to document things, including soft written confirmations.) As we saw in Chapter 4, it's also important to keep your tone of voice, expressions and body postures neutral and boring.

So as you disengage, don't gratify and educate an Emotional Predator by letting her see she's getting a rise out of you. Remain blank, unfazed, hard to read, bored, and perhaps even mysterious. Stick to bland facts. Even if you're not *feeling* disinterested, *display* disinterest (or, as we'll see when we look at misdirecting an Emotional Predator's attention, display an interest in what's not your real interest).

The second level of being unprovoked is to never make a decision while you're emotionally reactive. That requires recognizing when you're emotionally charged, an essential aspect of knowing yourself. Tune into the physical signs of being emotional like your pulse and breathing rates and sensations in your gut. Are you talking more animatedly, or faster or louder than you do when you're relaxed? And bear in mind that being emotionally charged often includes a feeling of urgency, a heightened impulse to respond right away. Acting in the heat of emotions is rarely wise. So when you suspect you're emotional, defer making any decisions. It's almost always okay to respond to a question or request by saying you're not sure and need time to consider things.

The third level of being unprovoked is to not have any internal emotional reaction at all. This is the holy grail of immunity, not easily or quickly achieved, so be kind to yourself if your emotions about an Emotional Predator aren't as even-keeled as you might like. When your inner experience isn't impacted by what she does and says, you're truly immunized and able to respond most effectively. To stop having internal emotional reactions, you'll need to change deeply held core values and beliefs. That takes time, courage and practice. Start by being kind to yourself, applying the Golden Rule Turned Inward, taking a long-term perspective, finding humor and practicing gratitude.

Again, the most important aspect of being unprovoked at any level is to *conceal* your emotional states from an Emotional Predator. To do that, know your emotional triggers, then *disconnect the lines between them and your emotional reactions*. Work toward being strategically responsive and emotionally unaffected.

Use Boundaries to Avoid Being Drawn into Engaging - An Introduction

An important part of disengaging from an Emotional Predator (and of protecting yourself if you stay engaged) is to set firm boundaries and stick to them. Chapter 7 looks at boundaries in detail, but they deserve an introduction here. A boundary with another person is a line or limit distinguishing acceptable from unacceptable behaviors from them. You draw that line by stating what you won't tolerate or participate in, and what consequences will follow from certain behaviors. Your boundaries should be based on what's real and makes sense *for you*, not on what an Emotional Predator says is real. Don't be intimidated into setting a boundary based on your fear of how she might react. Step outside her world and firmly establish boundaries that end or limit your interactions. Then don't be drawn into engaging more or re-engaging by relaxing your boundaries.

How you set your boundaries is as important as where you set them. In setting boundaries and all else, always communicate with an Emotional Predator without emotion (unless you're strategically displaying an emotion to mislead her about what's important to you). Being firm doesn't necessarily mean being harsh. You can be firm and polite and emotionless at the same time. And never set a boundary you aren't prepared to enforce.

When you're polite and unemotional, an Emotional Predator can't portray herself as your victim by complaining about your tone. Setting a boundary unemotionally also interferes with her efforts to transfer her emotional disturbance to you through projective identification. Sometimes it's useful to use the old "good cop/bad cop" ruse. Make social, legal or organizational rules, or your demanding schedule, the "bad cop" that sets the boundary for you and prevents you from going further. Relying on external rules whenever possible depersonalizes and shifts her focus away from you and onto the rules. It reduces the risk of a dangerous reaction from an exceptionally unhinged Emotional Predator. Chapter 7 discusses staying safe.

chapter seven

Step 5 - How to Deal Strategically with an Unavoidable Emotional Predator

Failing to prepare and plan is preparing and planning to fail.

"I believe that people make their own luck by great preparation and good strategy."
Jack Canfield

"Strategy is about making choices, trade-offs; it's about deliberately choosing to be different."
Michael Porter

PLAY EMOTIONAL PREDATOR GAMES BETTER THAN THEY DO

The strategy of avoiding and disengaging that we looked at in Chapter 6 may not be available or practical in your situation, particularly if the Emotional Predator is part of your family or at your work. As we saw, disengaging is really a special type of limited engagement for the purpose of avoiding a long term engagement, so we'll now revisit some tactics covered in Chapter 6 and add others. If you must, or if you choose to, remain involved with an Emotional Predator (you have children together, for example), it's vital to *be smart and strategic, and use effective tactics*, to protect yourself and your loved ones and restore the balance of power. Every strategy and tactic for dealing with an Emotional Predator, including disengaging, aims to re-balance power and restore control.

Many of the tactics for managing involvement with an Emotional Predator can be summed up as *playing the Emotional Predator's game better than she does and setting your own rules of engagement*. Don't bring a knife to a gun fight. Remember, playing her game better than she plays it doesn't make you an Emotional Predator. The tactics themselves may look the same and an uninformed observer may not readily distinguish between offensive and defensive uses, but there's a world of difference.

Control Information (an Introduction)

Controlling information is central to any strategy for protecting yourself. An Emotional Predator will carefully control the information she lets out, telling affirmative lies and distortions as well as lying by omission. This makes it important for you to mine all sources of information to get the facts and fill in what she's left out. Penetrate her facade by gathering information about her abusive, deceptive and manipulative behaviors and reality.

An Emotional Predator also will relentlessly try to mine you for information about you, particularly for information about what's emotionally important to you, what you hold near and dear to your heart, your core beliefs and values. So learn to play her hiding game better than she does by controlling the information you let out. The less she knows about you the better. Don't say what you *want* to say, say what will be *strategically smart* to say.

Like a good card player, remember that misleading your opponent is central to a good outcome. When an Emotional Predator thinks you care about things that are unimportant to you (and visa versa), she'll attack you where you're immune and not attack you where you're vulnerable. You can strategically mislead her both by withholding accurate information about you and by releasing inaccurate information. Although strategically faking an emotional display can put an Emotional Predator off balance and misdirect her attention, this tactic should be used sparingly and only by the theatrically inclined. Unless you're a good actor, it's probably better to remain emotionally invisible.

Many effective strategies are counter-intuitive, and our natural instincts and responses can make things worse. For example, your natural desire to be heard and have your experience validated can backfire badly when the Emotional Predator finds out what's important to you and uses it as leverage. Similarly, giving in to your desire to have him acknowledge his bad acts will betray you, because by definition, an Emotional Predator isn't capable of sincere remorse and guilt, and he'll use the insights you reveal about him to better hide his true nature.

Types, Sources and Direction of Information Flow

Managing the flow of information between you and an Emotional Predator, and with third parties, is part of almost all the strategies for protecting yourself. There are *three types* of information: information about yourself, about the Emotional Predator and about the situation. (Knowing about yourself is covered in Chapter 4.) In addition, information moves in *two directions*: you *acquire* it and you *release* it.

You can *acquire* information from *three sources*: from yourself, from the Emotional Predator and from third parties (which includes independent records). And you can *release* information to any of *three audiences*: to yourself, to the Emotional Predator or to third parties. Particularly when releasing information, but also when acquiring it, *involve third parties with caution.* Through ignorance or intention, third parties may or may not be trustworthy. Some could be helpful, others could be oblivious, still others could be enlisted now or in the future as Emotional Predator helpers or patsies.

This may sound more complex than it is. The bottom line is that effective protection from Emotional Predators involves controlling the information you reveal and acquire, taking into account what that information is, from whom it's acquired and to whom it's shared. Managing all the different types of information and the directions they flow is a central part of an effective defense, *but controlling the information you let out about yourself, particularly about your emotions, is essential.* If you wear your heart on your sleeve and let your emotional states be visible, there's little hope of effective protection. Common therapy admonitions to be open and honest and share your feelings are a disaster if you follow them with an Emotional Predator.

MASTERING THE EMOTIONAL PREDATOR GAME OF CONTROLLING INFORMATION - GATHERING INFORMATION

One part of controlling information is to gather it. The more you know, the more protected you'll be. Generally speaking you want information that can be used to identify and expose an Emotional Predator, such as evidence of disregard for others, lying by omission, and persistent selfishness. But you also want information that establishes the truth and information that can divert and mislead the Emotional Predator, such as identifying things he values. When you think about obtaining useful information about Emotional Predators (or about experts you're screening), keep in mind the traits, tactics, behaviors and attitudes of an Emotional Predator covered in Chapter 3.

Emotional Predators are the ultimate spin masters, using innuendo and lies of omission to distort and reverse reality. They can make even the most innocent things look dastardly. Just because you'd never use certain information to manipulate, just because you can't imagine how to distort and warp information to make it an instrument of manipulation, don't assume an Emotional Predator can't find ways to spin things to his advantage. So watch what he does and learn how he uses information to distort and manipulate others.

Know the Emotional Predator Better Than She Knows You and Better Than She Knows Herself

As we've seen, an Emotional Predator will try to know you better than you know yourself. She'll know your vulnerabilities and use them to manipulate and provoke you. So take that page from her play book, study her and know her better than she knows you and better than she knows herself. When you know her weaknesses, goals and patterns, you can find ways to sidestep her manipulations, expose her and provoke her to reveal her true nature.

It's always a good time to study an Emotional Predator. Be a sharp observer, while appearing to be disinterested. Use all three sources of information: yourself, the Emotional Predator and third parties. In particular, study yourself in reaction to her.

It can take considerable study to see things an Emotional Predator works hard to conceal, so don't be discouraged if a few observations don't yield a gold mine of information. Be patient. You're looking for the specific ways she *habitually* expresses the behaviors, thought patterns and responses common to Emotional Predators. How and with whom does she enact her compulsive drive to manage a positive appearance? Where can she be exposed? Is she lazy? Cheap? How is she hypocritical? What and who does she fear (does she fear running out of money, being laughed at, being scolded by an authority)? Where and with whom does she seek power and dominance? What does she assume (that her facade is working, that you aren't wise to her games, etc...)? What empty words or phrases does she use to dodge? How does she exercise any authority or power she has?

There are different ways to know. To become a sharp observer, cultivate as many as possible. Intellectual puzzle-solving is one way preferred in our culture, but it's not the only way and it may not be enough. Rationality can mislead us by rationalizing. Intellectualizing can move us away from feelings that carry important messages. And while it's important to listen to our feelings, that's not the same as letting them control us. In Chapter 4 we looked at Carl Jung's ideas about the importance of balancing information we get from what he called our four functions of consciousness: thinking; feeling; imagery (a.k.a. intuition) and sensation. To calibrate your own BS meter, tune into all of them.

Get the Facts

Because Emotional Predators repeatedly lie, asserting falsehoods and omitting truth, it's essential to become a fact-checker and detective. Don't accept things at face value. Be skeptical. Particularly when you hear an emotionally compelling story, ask yourself what might've been left out. Recognize when you're being gaslighted and seek out a wider range of information. Use forensic technologies to combat deep digital fakes.

To convince me that her ex-husband was disturbed, a mother told me a story in shocked and outraged tones of him soliciting men to join them in sex during their marriage. When I checked into it with her ex-husband and people who knew them as a couple, I found out that they *shared* an interest in having men join the two of them in sex, and that the wife had introduced this variation into their sex life. What she told me was true; her ex-husband had solicited men to join them. But she left out the crucial fact that she had initiated this and eagerly participated. Her introducing this variation is an example of a no-win bind set up. If he didn't go along, she'd blame him for being a prude. When he did go along, she later blamed him (using lying by omission) for being perverted.

There are many sources of useful information. Independent records, neutral people like teachers, co-workers, other parents and neighbors, and the Emotional Predator himself all can provide material for defending yourself. An Emotional Predator's social media posts can be a gold mine of useful information. You may be blocked, but you may know someone who isn't and who'd be happy to print and send you his revealing posts. Use internet and background searches, but be discerning; information on the internet can be astonishingly inaccurate and intentionally false.

When you're tapping neutral people for information about an Emotional Predator, be thoughtful about whether to let them know that's what you're doing. Having a spy can be invaluable, but if they know what you're after, they may not want to get involved - and they may confuse your use of the Emotional Predator tactic of mining for information with evidence that you're the problem.

In communications with the Emotional Predator or a third party, play dumb and misdirect their attention to unimportant issues. Feigning interest in matters that aren't important, while keeping alert to things that are, increases the odds that they'll let their guard down and reveal something useful.

One client of mine found out in a casual chat about sports with his ex-wife's neighbor that she'd been leaving the house alone after their pre-school children's bedtime. He already knew there was no other adult in her house, so he now realized that she was leaving the children alone. The neighbor wouldn't have knowingly betrayed his neighbor, so my client kept the conversation casual, and was careful to show no reaction to this alarming information. He also returned to secretly video her leaving with no lights on (hence no babysitter) when she had the children.

Be very careful before you try to get information from an Emotional Predator's children. Children have tremendous natural loyalty to parents, even abusive parents. They often tell an adult what they think the adult wants to hear. And trying to get information from your own children about their other parent risks putting them in the middle, which is commonly understood to be bad for children. Seeking information from your child about the other parent may offend your child's natural loyalty to both parents, particularly if you resort to leading questions that say or imply something negative about the other parent. That doesn't mean you can't and shouldn't *listen* carefully to what your children spontaneously say about their other parent, and *validate* their experience. Listening and validating a child's experience is different from interrogating and leading them to give you dirt. Quizzing your children for information about their other parent isn't likely to end well for them or you.

In summary, to combat an Emotional Predator's affirmative lies and lies of omission, you need the facts and context he's misstated and left out. Discovering those facts gives you a more complete and accurate understanding. And as you uncover facts and evidence counter to the story you've been told, document and organize what you uncover.

Document and Keep Good Records

Be sure to document and organize the information you gather. There's little point gathering information if you can't find what you need when you need it. Good records counteract gaslighting and expose an Emotional Predator when the time is right. Emotional Predators hate public exposure of their true nature. Using good records to pierce their facade of charm and innocence and bring their hidden behaviors out in the open is a good way to neutralize them and rally others to your defense. We'll look at that in the next section.

In addition to preserving evidence to show to others, keeping good records also helps you remember how badly the Emotional Predator has acted. Earlier we looked at the creative aspect of memory. As happens to victims of domestic violence, the target of an Emotional Predator can easily forget details because remembering can re-traumatize. The ex-husband of a client of mine, Heidi, took

$11,000 from her years earlier and admitted it at the time. For years after it happened, remembering this fact brought up a lot of hurt and anger for her, so she'd let it slip out of her memory. But back when it originally happened she carefully organized and saved the emails in which he clearly stated that he owed her the $11,000. Years later, when he claimed unfairness to him over minor expenses, Heidi was able to go back to her records and pull up the old emails she'd saved in which he admitted owing her $11,000. Re-reading those old emails helped ground her in the accurate history and avoid a gaslighting effect. Her records immunized her from his manipulative attempt to limit reality to only the narrow present and his appeals to her guilt over being "unfair" based only on current events fell on deaf ears.

Smart lawyers advise parents divorcing Emotional Predators to keep a journal of events, making entries as soon as possible after an incident. This kind of journal should record only events and facts, not your emotional reactions, opinions, thoughts, speculations or strategies. A journal of your personal reflections is different and should be kept separately.

A journal of events is one external storage medium that helps preserve history that you can't be expected to hold in memory, and might not want to remember because that prolongs your trauma. Other external storage media are recordings, photos, screen shots, emails and texts. In whatever media you choose, keeping saved materials organized makes it easier to later find what you need. Documentation that you can't find is worthless.

Of course, always be sure any records you make are completely safe from discovery by the Emotional Predator. Don't underestimate her capacity to pry and snoop. I've seen countless examples of

Emotional Predators hacking passwords, breaking into locked drawers and helping themselves to other peoples' personal and confidential information.

Part of controlling information and keeping good records is managing the media used to communicate. Emotional Predators love "he said, she said" situations where they can use their acting skills to sound persuasive. They'll say anything to get what they want, changing from moment to moment, conversation to conversation - and deny that they previously said something different. Conversations with an Emotional Predator that aren't independently documented might as well not have happened. He'll later deny what was said, or will recount the conversation with subtle changes that alter the meaning.

So, for practical purposes, if a communication with an Emotional Predator isn't recorded or witnessed, it didn't happen, or at least it didn't happen the way it actually happened. This is one reason (in addition to the risk of being emotionally provoked and, in extreme cases, the risk of violence) that conversations in person should be undertaken with caution. At a minimum, any verbal communication - in person or via telephone or video phone - should be recorded (subject to any limits of applicable law[33]) or witnessed. If you do have a verbal exchange with an Emotional Predator that wasn't electronically recorded or witnessed, write down your notes of what was said in a journal of events as soon as possible. *Contemporaneous* notes are deemed to be more accurate than things written down after time has passed.

For documenting bad behavior, hidden recording devices or witnesses are better than visible ones because an Emotional Predator will behave better if he knows he's being recorded or watched. And recordings may be better for documenting than witnesses. Witnesses later may be hard to get when you need them, but unless you mess up the technology, a recording should be there for you whenever you need it. And witnesses can be discredited as biased in your favor. Each situation is unique, so use your judgment and get advice from screened and trusted attorneys and counselors.

Particularly if you're at risk of being emotionally provoked, in most situations communicating in writing (usually via emails or texts) is better than communicating verbally, both for the written record it produces and for the time it affords you to compose and edit when you're calm and strategically alert. Divorced parents can do written messaging through a third party website like OurFamilyWizard.com or TalkingParents.com to ensure that all communications are "on the record."

On the other hand, although it can be treacherous to communicate verbally with an Emotional Predator, a recording of her being aggressive or overtly hostile can be good as gold. Two divorced parents told me diametrically opposite stories about what went on when they transferred their two year old daughter from one parent to the other, each blaming the other for being hostile. When one parent forwarded video and audio of three transfers taken from a home security camera, it was immediately clear which parent was honest and which wasn't.

If a picture is worth a thousand words, then an audio recording is worth a thousand pictures, and a video recording is worth a thousand audio recordings. Video recorders for home and car security and personal spying, and recording applications for smart phones, can catch an Emotional Predator's true nature. Recording technologies continually evolve, so keep up to date, or consult someone who is.[34] And be aware of the relevant laws.

In almost every case, recordings should be made without the Emotional Predator knowing she's being recorded. She's most likely to let down her charming facade in private, so try to catch a moment when she believes no one's looking. A client of mine used a small spy camera disguised as a bluetooth earpiece to record audio and video when he dropped off his children with ex-wife. She thought she was alone with him and behaved like the barbarian she truly was but kept carefully hidden from everyone except him. His recording of her screaming and ranting turned the tide of their court battle and forever immunized him and his children from her attacks.

Determining whether to try to record a verbal exchange depends in great part on whether you feel immune to emotional provocation and, perhaps, able to provoke the Emotional Predator. If the interaction would be in person, you also must assess whether there's a risk of violence. So consider recording only if you're confident that you can resist being provoked, and never engage in person unless you are safe. Usually a crowded public setting provides enough safety for a meeting, but each Emotional Predator and situation is unique, so assess your safety with the help of police and other security experts. Staying safe is discussed later in this chapter about behavior modification and boundaries.

For better or worse, we live in a James Bond sort of world where spying tools are readily available. Whenever possible, use these things to your advantage. But always bear in mind that the Emotional Predator may be recording *you* and that your written communications can be used against you. So always be calm, polite, unemotional and unprovoked in all your communications with an Emotional Predator, whether verbal or written.

Another effective way to document things is to get what I call *soft written confirmations* from people who've witnessed important things. In person, teachers, principals, coaches, co-workers, neighbors, and others will often tell you things that indict the Emotional Predator. But if you directly ask even a well-meaning third party to confirm what they told you, often they'll balk at being put on the record. Maybe understandably, most folks just don't want to get too involved as witnesses. I've seen a doctor omit from his medical record a child's clear description of his grandfather's violence toward him, because the doctor didn't want to "take sides." (Doctors are legally required to report child abuse.) Teachers see a lot, but they'll almost always refuse to "get involved" if you directly ask them to confirm something. Often that's school district policy.

So to document a third party's verbal report about an Emotional Predator (without resorting to secret recording), try an indirect, soft written confirmation. Soft confirmations work because, for most people most of the time, failure to deny something is taken to be assent and confirmation. So if you send someone a thank you note that mentions a useful thing they told you and they don't write back to correct you or deny saying it, then they have, in effect, confirmed it.

To do this skillfully, bury the statement that you want confirmed in a larger context (of thanking the other person for his time, for instance) and give no hint that his statement might be used against an Emotional Predator. A teacher may tell you in person that when your son comes from the other parent's house he's always upset and acting out and homework is rarely done. But the teacher is unlikely to put any of that in writing and may well deny he said it if pressed in front of other people. A soft written confirmation might be an email saying something like, "Dear Teacher Jones. Thank you for taking the time to meet with me about classroom materials and plans. [More words about materials and plans.] It was also helpful to hear that Johnny seems to have trouble in class when he's coming from his mom's house and that he doesn't seem prepared or fed on those days. I'll work with his mom on that." If the teacher doesn't write back denying that he told you those things, then the teacher has effectively confirmed them.

This technique of soft confirmation of facts also can be used in communications with an Emotional Predator, particularly with facts he's omitted. You slip in a fact he's omitted while the focus of your email is elsewhere. If he doesn't explicitly deny the fact, then for practical purposes he's admitted it. Soft confirmations misdirect attention the way focusing your questions on unimportant things does (we touched on that in Chapter 4).

Of course, soft confirmations also can be used against you, so you should always deny in writing any false written assertion made by an Emotional Predator. Something simple like "I don't agree," "I recall things differently," "that's not my understanding," or a similarly brief statement that you don't assent to what he reported is sufficient. As we'll see later in this chapter, choosing if, when and how to refute in detail an Emotional Predator's misstatements, distortions and omissions is a matter of strategy, and it's wise to not be provoked or drawn into *proving* the stupidity or inaccuracy of his assertions.

MASTERING THE EMOTIONAL PREDATOR GAME OF CONTROLLING INFORMATION - RELEASING INFORMATION

Know Your Audience: Emotional Predators and Others

The wisdom of knowing your audience and controlling what and how you share things with a particular audience can't be underestimated. Controlling what information you let out and to whom you let it out helps you regain power. Let's look at what and how to share things with an Emotional Predator before turning to other audiences.

When dealing with an Emotional Predator, pay careful attention to when, what and how you reveal things. Communicating openly and honestly with him is a trap for naive decent people. Be realistic about what the truth is and is not, and what it can and cannot do. The truth is your life line to your sanity, salvation and protection. The truth isn't a magic wand that changes an Emotional Predator.

Resist your desire to share what you know and what's true. It's a dangerous but seductive fantasy to believe an Emotional Predator will hear your truth, recognize it and change his ways, or to believe he'll understand, appreciate, respect, or acknowledge you for sharing what you know. He won't change who he is, become more self-aware, develop a conscience, or respect and appreciate you. He'll use information you reveal, even information you consider innocent and worthless, to improve his manipulations and better hide his true nature.

Confronting an Emotional Predator with her bad behavior is almost always among the worst things you can do. It just identifies you as a threat when you want to be as invisible as possible. There may be times when exposing an Emotional Predator *to others* is extremely helpful, but if she finds out, it alerts her to be more devious and keep you in her sights.

The non-verbal aspect of your communications often says more than your choice of words (which are also important). "I forgot" said in a sad tone and "I forgot" said sarcastically convey completely different messages. Whoever you're talking to, be aware of what your tone, facial expressions and body language reveal, and learn to control them. Remember, knowing other people's emotions is an Emotional Predator's stock in trade. So as a general rule, in dealing with an Emotional Predator, it's unwise to show emotions, non-verbally or through your word choices.

I say it's unwise to show emotions *as a general rule* because there may be times when an intentional strategic display of emotion can be useful to mislead an Emotional Predator. Appearing weak where you're strong and strong where you're weak is discussed toward the end of this chapter. But for the most part keep your emotions safely concealed.

You risk revealing yourself non-verbally in person and in telephone or live video communications. This means that, unless you're very skilled at managing your emotional reactions and are confident you can remain unprovoked, it's best to avoid those kinds of interactions and stick to written communications where only your choice of words can expose you - and you can think and edit before hitting "send" or posting.

And while it's easy to *talk* about controlling your expressions, it can be challenging to *actually* bring them under control, particularly when an Emotional Predator has already been messing with you. Whether your communications are verbal, non-verbal or written, to control them you need to know and detach from your emotional triggers to become immune to provocation. That circles us back to Chapters 4 and 5 about knowing yourself and loosening your grip on who you believe you must be.

In all your communications with an Emotional Predator: stick to just the facts; don't editorialize; don't characterize the Emotional Predator or the situation; don't state your opinion or feelings; use only neutral, boring language and emotionally bland tones; resist the urge to use sarcasm or put-downs; avoid adjectives, adverbs, and dramatic punctuation (!); and avoid absolute and emphatic words (like "never" and "always"). For example, although it may seem counter intuitive, "I forgot" is much more effective and powerful than "I *completely* forgot" or "I *totally* forgot". And "I have not done that" is more effective than "I have *never* done that."

And communicate in media you can save (i.e. writings or recordings); make direct, simple requests and only accept direct, clear answers; set clear benchmarks and deadlines, and clear consequences for failing to meet them; don't accept or believe excuses or statements of intention or plans; and never communicate in anger or frustration.

In addition to Emotional Predators, you can release information to third parties. (It's also true that *you* are a third audience for information, but opening yourself up to new ways of seeing things is covered elsewhere. Generally, you should always share everything you know with yourself. It's best to keep your eyes wide open, even to uncomfortable or alien things.)

Be thoughtful and strategic before revealing information to a third party who might later reveal things to an Emotional Predator. Emotional Predators gather information from innocent people around you - your friends, family, and neighbors, and your children's teachers, coaches, medical providers and therapists. So be a smart card player and don't show your cards to anyone the Emotional Predator might mine for information. In World War II, the public was reminded that "loose lips sink ships" because enemy spies could be anywhere. For the most part, unless a third party is confirmed to be safe from later disclosing things, remember Skipper the Penguin's advice and just smile and wave. When in doubt, *know it, don't show it*. The exception is when you *choose* to reveal specific information for the intentional purpose of having it get back to the Emotional Predator in order to mislead him.

Before you start confiding in someone, confirm that they're safe. At a minimum, a confidant must be outside of the Emotional Predator's sphere of influence. If you can find them and they aren't so traumatized that they've been overtaken by paranoia, other people who've been targeted by Emotional Predators - by your Emotional Predator, if available - sometimes can be a good source of emotional support and validation. Consider contacting his former spouses or partners. But be careful to avoid people who're still hypnotized by him or are as disturbed as he is. And know the difference between well-meaning acquaintances and true friends who'll tell you what you may not want to hear.

So knowing your audience and recognizing genuinely safe people is crucial. Sharing your experience *only* with trustworthy confidants helps you let off steam so you can stay calm and unreactive. It's also an antidote to the trauma of gaslighting. Verified safe confidants can shine light into dark corners where an Emotional Predator hides, exposing danger lurking there, validating your experience and cleansing your vision.

It's particularly natural, but dangerous, to want to believe that professionals can be trusted and will understand you. So carefully screen professionals (and anyone else you might confide in) to determine whether it's safe to share information with them, and if so how much to share. Your starting assumption, particularly with professionals and experts, should be that the other person won't understand the true nature of the Emotional Predator you are dealing with, and they may even be an Emotional Predator.

Screen Professionals and Experts

As we've seen, Emotional Predators are attracted to jobs where they can wield the power of expertise over others. They use positions of trust and authority as platforms for controlling and dominating. So the odds of encountering one in a helping profession, such as law and mental health, are greater than the odds of encountering one in the general population. This is equally true for mainstream and "alternative" professionals, mentors and gurus. In fact, "alternative" types may be more suspect because they tend to have less respect for rules. We comparative shop for home appliances, so don't hesitate to comparative shop for the best people to help with your interpersonal conflicts.

And even good hearted, well-meaning experts may not know how to deal with an Emotional Predator, although they may *think* they understand personality disorders and tell you they know what to do. *A well-intentioned professional helper embedded in an out of date cultural and mental health paradigm won't understand the true nature of Emotional Predators.* A professional may not get it, and worse, she may be an Emotional Predator herself.

So be cautious with professionals, mentors, gurus and other experts. Screen them for safety and usefulness before hiring or

STEP 5 - BE STRATEGIC | 201

confiding in them. Don't be intimidated to politely question authority. And don't mistake a professional for a good parent who'll make everything better.

But on the other hand, don't expect perfection from a professional. Emotional Predators sneak under even the best radar, and no expert is perfect or knows everything. Even a savvy professional who knows Emotional Predators and how to effectively defend against them occasionally can be caught off guard. Having been taken in by an Emotional Predator might make a professional particularly helpful, *if* being taken in has deepened her understanding. I've learned valuable lessons from Emotional Predators who've flown under my radar, and that schoolhouse never closes.

As you screen a professional helper (or anyone else), apply all the same techniques that you'd use to ferret out an Emotional Predator. No matter who you're screening, control the information you let out. Don't educate. Play dumb and make others demonstrate what they already know. Ask direct questions in neutral tones and language about hypothetical fact patterns. As we'll see later about *setting the rules of engagement,* control the location and media of exchange, and seek independent verification. And avoid leading questions where the answer you're looking for is suggested by the words or tone you use in your question.

Asking "You're an expert in dealing with personality disorders, aren't you?" is a leading question that won't distinguish good from bad professionals. It *supplies* more information than it's likely to produce. Hearing that leading question, an unhelpful professional will assure you they have the expertise about personality disorders you seek - whether they actually have it or not. "What are you an expert in?" is a more open-ended question (although it does reveal you're looking for expertise of some kind).

Don't be intimidated or befuddled by professional jargon or political correctness. A professional who uses jargon to obscure or impress, rather than clarify, or is politically correct or diplomatic to the point of evasion, isn't likely to help. Avoid experts who hide behind jargon, or don't answer direct questions with direct on-point answers. Their mystifying cloak of "expertise" blinds them too. When an expert fails to answer a direct question with a clear, on-point answer, it should raise at least a yellow flag warning. What are they dodging?

In Part 1, I described a highly regarded psychologist who assured me he knew how to handle personality disordered people. (Personality disorder is the diagnosis often applied to Emotional Predators.) Although warned before and as it was happening, he let an Emotional Predator mother wrap him around her finger, controlling the time and media of communications to thwart all efforts to get her son in to meet with him. I had to ask this psychologist three times whether he'd read George Simon's book *In Sheep's Clothing* before he gave a direct answer. The first two times, he dodged the question and assured me he knew all about its topic. After I repeated my simple, yes/no question a third time, observing that he hadn't answered the last two times, he finally admitted he hadn't read it - but still went on to tell me what was in it.

Along with asking direct questions, to test whether an expert (or anyone else) really understands Emotional Predators and cuts through the crap, try using open-ended questions about hypothetical fact patterns. I screened a new school counselor, another therapist who claimed to know all about personality disorders, this way. To assess what she really knew, I described a hypothetical parent's bedtime routine for a pre-school child and asked the counselor for her thoughts about it.

Here's the hypothetical bedtime routine I made up. After brushing teeth, etc, ... a parent put a child into his bed. The parent then set a loud egg timer alarm for five minutes and read aloud until the alarm went off. The parent then reset the alarm for five more minutes, turned off the light and sat on the floor of the room. When the alarm went off the second time, the parent left the room. The parent read for five minutes, sat for five minutes and left, with both five minute periods ending in a loud egg timer alarm. If the child had dozed off during the reading period, when the first alarm went off, it woke him up. And if he fell asleep during the second five minute period, the alarm marking its end woke him up. Either way, the parent's bedtime routine was assured to *wake* the child and leave him *awake*. Once the parent left, they wouldn't return.

Non-professionals who've heard this hypothetical routine easily identified it as shockingly selfish and lacking empathy for the child. But when I asked the school counselor what she thought of it and what it said about a parent who'd do this, the counselor *side-stepped and refused to answer*. First she simply ignored the question, offering only *vague jargon* about "following up," "connecting" and "being open and present." When I pressed for the counselor's opinion about that bedtime routine, even embellishing the hypothetical to add that a psychologist's report had described the egg timer parent as exhibiting several traits found in personality disorders, the counselor *became peevish, petulant and haughty*, and still refused to answer. Side-stepping and refusing to answer, offering vague jargon, and becoming peevish, petulant or haughty are red flag warning signs that a person isn't safe. I found out what I needed to know by paying as much attention to what she did not say as to what she did say.

So in summary, carefully screen professionals and other mentors, gurus, helpers (and confidants), using the same tests you'd use to ferret out an Emotional Predator. Play dumb, ask direct but neutral open-ended questions in detached tones, ask about hypothetical fact patterns, and don't suggest the answers you seek from the way you pose your questions. When in doubt about a professional, avoid them, or at least get a second (and maybe third) opinion.

And consider whether you really need professional help at all. In some situations, you might be better off saving your money for positive rejuvenating experiences for yourself and your family. But sometimes professional help is necessary, usually when you're entangled in the legal system. In those situations, *carefully screened* lawyers, therapists, and evaluators can be essential allies.

After Screening, Disclose Selectively and Wisely

Sharing what you know and feel and have been through with truly safe and neutral third parties - folks you've carefully screened - can be helpful and reassuring. But bear in mind that third parties can be well-intentioned but unwitting dupes - or, worse yet, allies - of an Emotional Predator. Emotional Predators recruit others to feed them information and do their dirty work, and sometimes they band together to dominate.

So be selective when you pick people to reveal things to - about an Emotional Predator, yourself or anything else. In particular, be strategic about when and to whom you expose an Emotional Predator. Is there a greater authority to whom the Emotional Predator will defer? Does he fear certain authorities more than others: teachers, police, work supervisors, judges, custody evaluators, priests?

If you choose to expose an Emotional Predator, *share his behaviors, not your diagnosis or analysis of his behaviors.* Let what he does speak for itself, and keep in mind that his speech is a form of behavior. Don't be subtly provoked into sharing your conclusions. It's natural to want to share your truth based perhaps on years of experience, but it's more effective to simply share facts and let the other person draw their own conclusions. And the strongest way to present facts is through independent documentation.

Few people will have enough time or attention to hear all the details, and few will accurately understand the nature of the beast or the meaning of events. So don't regale anyone with long stories or lots of documents, unless you first get permission. Use one or two clear and well documented examples of bad behavior, and let your listener know you have more if they want them. This demonstrates your sensitivity to their limited time and attention. Even experts have a limited tolerance for hearing your war stories. If your listener doesn't understand Emotional Predators, refer them to good books (endnote 32 lists my favorites).

It's particularly tempting to want to tell what you know to people who have power and authority over the Emotional Predator, like a custody evaluator or judge, or people who can be persuasive witnesses, such as a teacher, coach or principal. But their position alone doesn't make them a good audience. Custody evaluators, therapists and judges in particular like to be the wise one - it's part of their identity as an expert. With authorities (and others), you can end up looking like a judgmental problem when you tell them your diagnoses, labels or negative conclusions about an Emotional Predator, or let your opinion leak through in your tone or expression. So when your audience is an authority, even though you may know more than they do, let them be the expert (or a least let them think they are).

To summarize, when you share things about an Emotional Predator with others, choose your audience wisely. Then just present the naked documented facts of selected examples, play more ignorant than you are, and let others reach the conclusion that you reached years ago. Let your audience have their satori moment of seeing how the facts expose the Emotional Predator's abuse and manipulation. Your focus should be on her behaviors, not on any quality of her person or psyche, not on her diagnosis, and not on any moral judgment or stance.

When the Time is Right, Use Your Documentation to Expose the Emotional Predator

Knowing what you know about an Emotional Predator is important, but rarely enough. When you have good records of the relevant facts and his bad behaviors, you're in a position to expose him. Having documentation ready doesn't mean it's strategically wise to do so. It might be smarter to hold that ammunition in reserve to be used at the right moment.

Emotional Predators can waste your time and resources with little effort on their part. It takes an Emotional Predator a minute or two to dash off an email of delusional accusations and wild distortions. But refuting every bogus assertion he makes can take hours of your time, and cost a lot in attorney fees. You might have to review, organize, quote, and cut and paste old emails, or contact old associates. Proving the negative - that you *never* said or did something - can be nearly impossible. And sometimes trying to refute an absurd accusation makes the accusation sound more plausible. Although as we saw about soft confirmations an assertion not denied is usually taken as confirmed, a truly stupid assertion may not merit a reply, or may merit only something to the effect that the assertion is too silly to merit a reply.

Rather than trying to disprove an Emotional Predator's vague or undocumented accusation, ask *him* to provide specific affirmative proof. That usually either shuts him up because he has none, or elicits more information from him as he tries to build his case. You may later need to refute bogus accusations and assertions with documented facts - for your own sanity or for the benefit of someone like a judge, boss, family members or custody evaluator - but it's better to do this when you choose, not when you're reacting to a mindless and disorienting provocation.

So instead of refuting an accusation the moment it arrives, it's often best to just deny it as briefly as possible ("I disagree" or "that's not true" are often sufficient), ask for specific proof, and maybe concisely summarize the facts - then leave proving the truth for the right moment. In the meanwhile, you can ponder what his accusations tell you about his tactics and state of mind. Often an Emotional Predator's accusations are projections that are properly understood as statements about himself.

But plan ahead. Take the time to document things in an organized way as they happen, so you can quickly marshal those resources when you truly need them. Then when you want to refute false assertions, the material you need will be at your fingertips. Many times, it's a matter of cutting and pasting old emails you've stored in a well labeled file into a single new email, and then re-sending that email as often as needed. Recall Heidi, the woman who was able to find old emails from her ex-spouse admitting he'd taken $11,000 from her.

Strategically using your documentation and communications is part of playing an Emotional Predator's game better than he does. Out-manage appearances by leaving a paper trail that makes you look good while exposing him. When you're on record consistently acting and communicating in mature, respectful ways, you look good. On the other hand, being emotionally reactive, frustrated and angry makes you look bad and is what the Emotional Predator will work to provoke in you. Make wise choices about when and how (and to whom) to disclose information.

Other Disclosure Tips

And in addition to letting documented facts about the Emotional Predator's bad behaviors speak for themselves, you gain credibility with third parties when you also say something positive about the Emotional Predator. Sometimes all you can offer is something minor or trivial. The unstated message of that kind of back-handed compliment, is that this is the *only* positive thing that can be said. Let the listener think, "If that's the best he can say about her, then she must be pretty bad." A father got that response by answering an evaluator's question about his ex-wife's strengths as a parent by saying in a positive way, "she likes to play board games with the children once a week and the children enjoy that."

While it's true that, except in rare moments, telling the truth to an Emotional Predator is self-defeating, occasionally it can be useful to reveal some truth to an Emotional Predator in order to misdirect her focus and attacks, or let her know you have the power to expose her. But for the most part, telling the truth to an Emotional Predator just tells her how to more effectively hide and manipulate.

Sharing information with an Emotional Predator also can draw you into an unwinnable "debate" which drains you to the core and leaves you emotionally violated. Remember, arguing with a crazy person is crazy. So be *situation specific* with what you reveal, and always be mindful of *how* you're saying whatever you choose to say. *Communications with an Emotional Predator are opportunities to gain information and mislead her, not educate her or get her sympathy.* If you play dumb and misdirect her attention to unimportant issues, you'll increase the odds that she'll let her guard down about an important subject and reveal useful information. These strategic choices become easier the more you know about yourself and your triggers and, thus, the less reactive you are.

MORE WAYS TO OUTPLAY EMOTIONAL PREDATORS AT THEIR OWN GAME

Provoke Them When You Can

Taking a page from an Emotional Predator's play book, learn what provokes *him* to explode, be an otherwise visible jerk or reveal too much. If you know what provokes him, when the right moment arrives, you can get him to expose himself with his own emotional reaction. But don't confuse strategically provoking him with letting yourself be provoked into retaliating in kind. Don't lash out. If you need to vent (and anyone dealing with an Emotional Predator needs to vent) do that in the safety of a screened therapist's office or with a proven safe friend.

In looking for things that might provoke an Emotional Predator, consider that *he's likely to be provoked by the things he does to try to provoke others*. Observe him to identify the tactics he uses that you can use against him. For example, Emotional Predators provoke with passive aggression. If you can overcome your decent instinct that it's bad to ignore someone or deny them what they need or deserve, you can use the powerful tool of passive aggression against an Emotional Predator. Denying him what he wants in an agreeable way, delaying your responses, and ignoring him and his requests, are forms of his passive aggressive games you can put to use.

If you decide to provoke, be sure you look good to everyone else. Always leave an impeccable record of being calm and reasonable in your behaviors and communications. As we saw when looking at recording Emotional Predator behaviors, always assume you're being recorded. It'd be self-defeating to be recorded acting like an ass in order to provoke an angry reaction. Whatever the reason, if you act like an ass, you're an ass. So stay publicly cool, calm and collected.

Set the Rules of Engagement – Manage When, Where and What

Set your own rules of engagement with an Emotional Predator. Control when, where and what as much as possible. There may be times when it's strategic to agree to an Emotional Predator's media, time and place, or agenda, either to make her mistakenly believe she's in control, or because it's not really important and would be a wasteful distraction to fight over (it's, as they say, not a hill to die on). Other times it may be strategic to stand firm about when, where and what, perhaps to frustrate and provoke her or to distract her into fighting over these *process* choices when your real interest is in the content.

Appearing to care about something you don't care about (like when, where or how you engage) can be an effective way to misdirect an Emotional Predator's attention. She'll do her best to drain your energy and get you chasing your tail or running after irrelevant things. Use that tactic against her. Let her waste efforts dealing with things that aren't really important to you, leaving her less energy to fight about the things that are.

Controlling the use of *time* is a subtle but significant exercise of power that can be more effective than you might think. So don't let an Emotional Predator rush you into things and don't accept unreasonable delays. At the very least, document these things when they happen. For example, a simple email like "I asked you two weeks ago and you haven't answered" may not get an answer, but it documents the delay for exposing her in the future. And as long as it doesn't make you look like the problem, use delay and rushing to put her off balance.

As we've seen, delaying your responses is a form of passive aggression, which is a page out of the Emotional Predator play book that can be effective for you. Although an Emotional Predator will demand immediate responses to what he wants, in almost every case it can wait (and of course, he'll take his time getting back to you when it serves him). An attorney who'd delayed his responses for months sent me an email demanding I give him an answer "within 48 hours" to a question that had no inherent deadline. He underlined "within 48 hours" as part of his attempt to intimidate and bully me, as though his adamant demand somehow required that I immediately jump to satisfy him on his schedule. I wrote back that I was busy and couldn't give him a thoughtful response within 48 hours, and that if time permitted I'd get to it the following week. When I set this rule of engagement for the timing of our interaction, he backed off and I didn't hear from him again about it.

The unspoken and real message I sent him in this exchange over timing was that he didn't control or dominate me. By setting this boundary about timing I also gained information. His failure to follow up confirmed my suspicion that his question itself was just a ploy to test for dominance and his real purpose was to see if he could intimidate me, using timing as the test. Noticing the power dynamic an Emotional Predator embeds in his communication (in this case his demand for an answer "within 48 hours") often tells you as much or more than the content. Put another way, the *context* of an Emotional Predator's communications can reveal more than the *content*.

When you can, delay and patiently let out rope with which the Emotional Predator can hang himself, while keeping your eye on the long term, big picture and waiting until the situation is ripe for directly exposing or opposing him. When he doesn't get what he wants right away, he's likely to become agitated and ramp up his demands and tactics. This makes him more visible.

The father of a teenager I'd begun treating started with reasonably civil emails asking me for things of no objective urgency. When I didn't respond right away, the father started sending more curt, less polite demands. That shift in tone put me on alert, so I tested by delaying a bit more (with a polite email explaining I wouldn't be able to respond until after the weekend). This elicited sarcastic and accusing emails, which were part of confirming the father's true Emotional Predator nature.

You may lose the advantage of surprise if you engage about something too soon. The moment you start responding to a particular issue or bad behavior, you alert the Emotional Predator to focus on that issue or behavior. Delaying your response can lull him into relaxing and believing that you're not going to oppose him (a form of misdirecting his attention). Sometimes just strategically timing your response and taking action when least expected is enough to throw him off balance (something he'll try to do to you).

Letting yourself be rushed is a form of being provoked. Don't be drawn into reacting on his schedule. Don't take the emotional bait. Don't let an intense feeling that you need to reassert yourself or your reality confuse you into thinking that the issue or question he's thrown at you is truly important or urgent.

Slowing down helps you monitor your emotions and be less emotionally reactive. Responding with something like, "I don't know. I'm not sure. I'll think about it and get back to you" is a simple and effective way to regain control by putting the timing and pace of communications on your terms. Appearing ignorant or confused - another game Emotional Predator's play - is a good way to justify taking more time to "look into it" or "do some research" or "think about it."

An Emotional Predator will wear you down with stupid, ir-relevant stuff that you should ignore. If you don't, you'll soon find yourself exhausted and your energies frittered away on distractions. Conserve your energy, money and resources, and marshal them for the most efficient time to use them. For example, witnesses can't be counted on to speak up over and over again. And once a witness has been used, the Emotional Predator will be on guard to conceal from her, and undermine or even attack her. Wait to use witnesses and other resources until they'll be most effective and the stakes are worth it. Choose your battles.

So be patient. Wait until something you know to be truly impor-tant is at stake. Wait until your resources, like money, documented examples and witnesses, are available. Wait until you can surprise the Emotional Predator. Wait until he visibly ramps up his demands. Wait until the situation is ripe for exposing him to third parties who hold power and authority. But, of course, don't ignore Court or other legal deadlines without advice from a good attorney.

If you're going to meet with an Emotional Predator or someone in their orbit, give some thought to the *location* of the meeting. For example, meeting someone in a public setting can distract, relax and disarm them and restrain abusive behaviors. I set the location of my initial meeting with the new school counselor mentioned earlier in this chapter at a coffee shop, rather than her office or my office. The more casual setting helped lower her guard, while taking her out of her "home court." Standing your ground about where you'll interact can send a powerful message.

As part of setting the rules of engagement, sometimes it's also useful to clearly limit in advance the *topics* you're willing to discuss. Set the agenda you're willing to engage about and stick to it, unless you're confident that deviating serves your interests. An Emotional Predator may try to divert communication off topic for a number of reasons, for example to distract from his bad behaviors or put you on the defensive or off balance. If you keep to only the topic you have agreed to discuss, and end the communication if he wanders to other topics without your consent, you do much to re-balance power between you.

Manage the Appearances You Present

Managing appearances is another useful page to take from an Emotional Predator's play book. So maintain the most likable, unthreatening persona possible, without being phony. Whether it's with the Emotional Predator or third parties (unless they are *proven* trustworthy allies), you should always use calm neutral language. Never use sarcasm or insults, no matter how badly you feel provoked. Save venting your true feelings for proven safe confidants. When appropriate, use media and social media smartly, but beware of trying to out-maneuver an Emotional Predator on social media. If you can afford it, hire a marketing or public relations person to help you cultivate a positive image on the internet and in traditional media.

First impressions can have more influence than you might want to believe. For better or worse, most people make judgments based on superficial and initial impressions, and once a judgment is made, it's hard to reverse. With new people, an Emotional Predator will try to create a first impression of you before you get there. In new situations like a new school year, starting a custody evaluation, or getting a new boss, try to establish a connection with new people before an Emotional Predator in your life does. Let the new person know you as a decent, honest person so when the Emotional Predator later tries to vilify you and play your victim, the new person won't buy it. But don't try to build yourself up by tearing the Emotional Predator down.

A person who says bad things about someone else, even if they're true and documented, can end up looking like the bad guy, or at least half of the problem, and the true bad guy ends up playing the victim of having bad things said about him. Be cautious about sharing too much about your Emotional Predator, even documented facts, too early in a new relationship. When you do share documented facts with a new person, if you add your negative opinions, characterizations or diagnoses, the new person is likely to think you're "negative" and see you as part or all of the problem. It's best to show yourself to be empathetic, considerate, positive and helpful. Gradually, let the facts speak for themselves. Let the Emotional Predator look bad by saying bad things about you to someone who already knows you as considerate, good and kind.

Use a Lull in the Action

Emotional Predators are expert at lulling you into a sense of false security by presenting a temporary facade of mellowness, reasonableness or cooperation. Don't be fooled. *Good behavior from an Emotional Predator is always in furtherance of future selfish bad behavior.* It's laying the foundation for a future manipulation. So, as Mad Eyed Moody admonished his pupils at the Hogwarts School, "constant vigilance!" Don't let an Emotional Predator lull you into false security by appearing to have changed into a decent person. It's not paranoid to keep your guard up even during seemingly pleasant interactions and keep your guard at least on standby during quiet periods. But don't show you're on guard.

Emotional Predators will be cooperative, friendly, even generous and helpful whenever they think it serves them - but only as long as they think it serves them. They will be obstructive, hostile, aggressive and stingy again as soon as they think that serves them. So don't count on a period or moment of apparent decency continuing after it becomes inconvenient or unproductive for the Emotional Predator. Emotional Predators are always scheming or positioning themselves even when they appear dormant. If they never again attack or pull a devious manipulation, it's because they see no benefit to them, or they know you're well-defended and attacking you would cost them more than they'd gain, or they've moved on to other easier prey. It's not because they've changed who they are.

A lull in aggression from an Emotional Predator is a good time to disengage emotionally and, as much as possible, practically and logistically. Use any break in the action to organize your documentation, re-connect with old interests and engagements, create new separate interests and supportive relationships, and move on. Building a supportive network of friends and fortifying activities is a great antidote to the poison of an Emotional Predator.

Be Skeptical of Emotional Predators' Out of Character Good Deeds

Never underestimate the lengths an Emotional Predator will go to in order to distort and manipulate. And if she does something helpful or cooperative that's out of character, be skeptical. There's almost always a hidden selfish or manipulative motive. A client, Alan, told me about an incident that illustrates this. It first struck me as so outrageous and improbable that I doubted his story. But after confirming what he told me by reading the emails and court documents and talking with people at the medical clinic where it took place, this incident helped me to understand the importance of never underestimating the extent to which an Emotional Predator will lie, deceive and manipulate.

Alan's ex-wife routinely left the logistical task of scheduling their child's appointments to Alan. But uncharacteristically, one time she volunteered to schedule the child's followup doctor appointment. Alan naively interpreted this as a sign that she was changing and finally taking responsibility for getting things done for the child. Alan thought she was finally being a decent helpful person, *something he dearly wanted*. He saw what he wanted to see.

But at the appointment, things unfolded in a bizarre way. As Alan later learned, the mother had set up the doctor's appointment as part of a larger scheme to try to take full control of the child by making Alan look bad. She manipulated the staff at the doctor's office to lay a foundation for her later power grab. It's worth looking closely at the details of this incident to see how things that seem innocent on the surface, or out of character for an Emotional Predator or bizarre, might fly under our radar taken separately. But taken together, they can expose what an Emotional Predator is really up to.

The mother chose to make the follow up appointment with a branch office where she would have the initial contact with the staff. *Initial impressions are important.* When she set up the appointment, she told the staff that the father would be attending and then lied about him. In the guise of warning and protecting them, she told the staff that Alan had untreated mental illness which made him violent and dangerous, all of which she knew was untrue. She told them that the doctor and security staff should be on guard against violence from him.

The mother knew these allegations weren't true because she'd made them ten years earlier during their divorce (when she'd first tried to take total control of the child), and they'd been thoroughly investigated by a psychologist and found false. The mother knew from that investigating psychologist's detailed report that Alan had no mental illness and was not violent or dangerous. But ten years later, she intentionally told this *emotionally alarming,* but thoroughly false, story to the new clinic staff. She did this to set up a hostile response from the clinic staff to Alan, counting on them to see what they expected to see.

At the appointment, the doctor behaved bizarrely. He was jumpy, jittery and agitated. He started by saying he'd just read the child's file, which was in his lap. Then he asked the parents for the date of the original injury. When neither parent remembered, Alan pointed out that the injury date was in the file on the doctor's lap (that the doctor said he'd just read). Instead of opening the file and looking, the doctor repeated the question. Bizarre.

When both parents again said they didn't know, Alan again asked the doctor to look in the file. The doctor, clinic director and security guard later confirmed to me that Alan didn't raise his voice or move his body or do anything aggressive or threatening. He was slumped down in his chair in a passive, tired posture. He just asked the doctor a second time to look in the file.

But the doctor suddenly jumped up, pointed at Alan and yelled "You're agitated! I'm calling security!" and bolted out of the room. The mother's dire fictitious warnings had set the doctor to expect violence from the father. *The doctor saw the father that he expected to see, not the father who was actually there.* Alan, for his part, was utterly baffled and thought the doctor was having some kind of nervous breakdown. (The mother, of course, knew that her plan was executing as she'd hoped.) The clinic director and security guard came in, reviewed events in front of the parents and found nothing out of the ordinary in Alan's behavior. The mother then left with the child.

The clinic director apologized to Alan for the doctor running out without finishing the appointment. Alan and the security guard shared a few laughs, with the security guard shaking his head at the doctor's behavior and also apologizing for it. Not realizing the doctor's bizarre behavior had been caused by the mother's manipulative lies, *Alan thought little more about it*, except that the doctor might need help. Only later did Alan and the clinic staff realize that the mother had set up the doctor to be afraid of a harmless father. But that was only the first part of her larger scheme.

The mother's devious plan only came to light a few months later when she filed a motion in the court seeking to take full control of the child and cut the child off from Alan. Her motion was based on the same baseless and discredited, but alarming, allegation she'd made ten years earlier: that he was violent and dangerous because of an untreated mental illness. In textbook Emotional Predator fashion, *she asserted as true things that had been clearly documented as untrue*, in this case in the exhaustively researched psychologist's report from her divorce.

In her motion, the mother presented as "evidence" that the child had been prevented from getting medical care at that doctor's appointment because, she alleged, the father had "become violent" and "been escorted off the premises by security." She told the court these lies about what had actually happened, *lying by omission* again (it was *partly* true that the appointment hadn't been finished) to create an emotionally compelling plausible but completely false story. Emotional Predators will create a fabricated story like this, built on an edifice of prior lies and situations they've gone to great lengths to set up.

When Alan read the mother's court motion, he started making connections and he began researching what had really happened at the clinic. He contacted the clinic director and learned what the mother told the staff when she set up the appointment. From this research, he learned that the mother's blatant but emotionally alarming lies had put the doctor in a state of mild terror, anticipating violence from the father. The doctor's bizarre behavior now made sense as a manipulated response to the mother's frightening lies. After re-reading emails and the psychologist's report from his divorce, Alan realized that the entire affair at the clinic, starting with the mother's *out of character volunteering* to set up the appointment, was part of a carefully planned manipulative plot that the mother had enacted over many months. Her offer to be "helpful" by scheduling the appointment was part of her devious scheme to grab power and possession of the child.

This example teaches that *when you're dealing with an Emotional Predator, or suspect you might be dealing with one, don't accept out of character or apparent good deeds at face value. Emotional Predator's never do things for others unless they think it will benefit them*. Be skeptical. Research for omitted facts and evidence counter to the story you've been told. Notice who's made first contact with new people. If you're not sure whether the person you're dealing with is an Emotional Predator or has been manipulated by one, look beneath the surface of things to determine what's really going on and whether the person is, or is not, an Emotional Predator.

Remember that Skepticism is Prudent, Not Paranoid

Being skeptical about other people and their intentions isn't paranoid, it's prudent. To see through the charming, seductive or innocent facade of an Emotional Predator, you have to stretch your imagination, do research, and be doubting. If you're told a plausible emotionally compelling story that elicits your sympathy, ask yourself what additional information and back-story might reverse your sympathies. If a storyteller says someone treated them badly, ask yourself what the storyteller might've done to provoke the person they're accusing and what independent evidence might say about the big picture.

Don't take things at face value. Be an investigative reporter and dig quietly to get the underlying history and facts. It's often revealing to ask the person being accused and denigrated for their side of the story and to find out whether the story you were told about them left out any background, history or facts. Seek independent documentation. Use common sense and consult others with good judgment who are uninvolved and have the courage to speak plainly and honestly to you. And recognize your fantasies about who someone is or who you want them to be, and about who *you* are and who you think *you* should be.

Prudence isn't paranoia. Caution isn't cynicism. Skepticism isn't unfair. And being prudent, cautious and skeptical also isn't losing sight of the many wonderful people all around you. Be alert to your environment and take appropriate precautions. When crossing a glacier, it's wise to rope up, even if it later turns out that there actually weren't any crevasses hidden under the surface snow. When moving through a social environment that may have Emotional Predators lurking in it, it's wise to be alert and take precautions too. Better safe than sorry.

A word about trust. Like the word love, trust can mean different things. Trusting in the sense of *counting on consistent behaviors* is different from *opening yourself and being emotionally vulnerable* to someone else. In the sense of counting on consistency, you can *trust* that Emotional Predators will act consistent with the selfish traits, drives and behaviors described in this book. You can trust that they'll always put themselves first and so on. But trusting an Emotional Predator in the sense of exposing yourself and making yourself emotionally (or financially) vulnerable is a different matter. Let people *earn* your emotional (and financial) trust. Place your emotional trust carefully - and only after you've observed and probed for background facts that provide context and a fuller understanding of who the other person is. When you meet people, be open to being pleasantly surprised over time, but be prepared for disappointment.

You can trust that Emotional Predators will acknowledge and do only what they think will serve their interests. When they do acknowledge or do something that appears to offer them no obvious benefit, be skeptical and look beneath the surface for the hidden benefit they see in it for themselves. Sometimes what they're really after isn't so obvious. Looking closely at the possible selfish benefits that an Emotional Predator is after helps you understand and fend off a future manipulative maneuver. Particularly in the early stages of dating, but in other phases of relationships as well, a naively trusting person will believe another person's story until it's proven untrue. But a wise person will remain skeptical until the other person is proved emotionally and otherwise trustworthy.

DEFENSE TACTICS FOCUSING ON BEHAVIOR MODIFICATION AND BOUNDARIES

Reward Good Behavior and Sanction Bad Behavior

A simple behavior modification approach can be useful with Emotional Predators. When opportunities present themselves, punish an Emotional Predator's bad acts with negative consequences and reward his good acts with positive consequences. These basic tenets of behavior modification play directly to an Emotional Predator's obsession with his self-interest as he perceives it.

A punishment denies the Emotional Predator something he wants or imposes something he does not want. It could be as simple as disengaging and disappearing, which deprives him of the feeling that he's having some impact or influence on you. Or it could be public exposure.

Learning about the specific things an Emotional Predator wants teaches you which negative consequences are likely to have the most impact. If he feels important when you cook for him, try refusing to cook for him until he changes a behavior. If he craves weekly phone calls with you, he may behave better when faced with losing those calls.

Emotional Predators always want to look good to others. This means that exposing, or threatening to expose, their poor behavior can be a powerful negative consequence. Sometimes just threatening exposure is enough because they see behaving better as the path of least resistance that lets them keep a good appearance. Other times, it takes actual public exposure. Publicly exposing an Emotional Predator might produce an aggressive reaction. But odds are that would be temporary because it likely would expose him even more, which in turn would reinforce the negative consequence of exposure.

In addition to an Emotional Predator's need to look good, leverage his need to dominate which drives him to attack what's important to you. Divert his focus and direct his attacks to something you pretend to care about, but in truth have little or no interest in. Reward him by letting him believe he's won something important to you, that you've sacrificed in exchange for his better behavior. Whether you appeal to what the Emotional Predator wants and values, or you offer a false target of something you pretend to value, never lose sight of what drives him.

When punishing bad behavior with negative consequences, try to leave the Emotional Predator a way to *save face* as she backs off. Backing a wild animal into a corner is dangerous. Remember, Emotional Predators crave feeling dominant and winning. They view life as a zero-sum game in which one person's win is another person's loss - and they can't tolerate feeling like they've lost, or that you've won. So whenever possible leave the Emotional Predator a way to improve her behavior that she can accept as good for *her* and in *her* interests. All you need to do is offer her a way for her to *call it* a "win" - or at least not a "loss" - for her. Don't let your pride or emotional wounds drive you to seek a result that has you labeled as the "winner" or dominant over her. Changing her behavior is enough. Let her feel she wins by improving her behavior, or at least that she doesn't lose.

Remember What Drives an Emotional Predator and Appeal Only to That

In all things related to Emotional Predators, always keep in mind that *they are driven only by what serves them and their need to domi-nate and control.* Don't lose sight of this critical truth. An Emotional Predator patient of mine, who'd twice been diagnosed as a sociopath, confirmed this to me, candidly stating that only the threat of some-thing bad for him (in that instance the threat of having his parole revoked) had any meaning for him.

His wife had spent a half hour pleading with him to stop his drug dealing because of the threat it presented to her and their children, including the risk that their home could be impounded, leaving her and their children homeless. As her pleas got more and more ani-mated and emotional, both of them grew more and more frustrated. When she finally blurted out that if he didn't stop, she'd have to report him to his parole officer and have him sent back to prison, everything changed. He immediately exhaled with relief, then blurted out, "Why didn't you just say that in the first place? Okay. I'll stop." Then, exasperated, he explained that "all that talk about you and the kids doesn't mean anything to me." He said this with no shame, remorse or embarrassment, but as a plain statement of the obvious (to him) fact that any dummy should know. When I asked him if I was understanding him correctly that talk of the impact on others had no meaning to him, but talk of the negative consequence to *him* was something he could understand, *with great relief for being understood*, he told me "Yes. Of course. Thank you." Other Emotional Predators may not be as candid, but they operate the same way.

With an Emotional Predator, appeals to "fairness," "what's good for the children" (or anyone else), "reasonableness," "decency" or anything other than what he wants for himself are meaningless. Appealing to any of these things which make sense *to you* serves only to instruct him about things you value. So if you're going to try to convince him to behave better, appeal to his self-interest as he perceives it.

Set Boundaries and Stick to Them

Enforcing boundaries is an important form of behavior modification that we touched on in Chapter 6. Emotional Predators regularly challenge, push and ignore other people's personal boundaries and the collective boundaries set by the rules of society. They count on good people tolerating this.

You find out a lot about another person when you set firm boundaries. Decent people will respect and accept your boundary graciously and without fuss. If they stray over your boundary, they'll acknowledge it and try to accommodate you. But restrained by your boundary, an Emotional Predator will become unhappy and agitated and redouble her efforts to get past it. She'll resort to a variety of manipulations to weaken your boundary, like trying to induce guilt by playing the victim and accusing you of being the problem, or flashing anger to intimidate you, or charming you to seduce you. And she won't acknowledge her violation. When an eleven year old set a boundary around not having his lunch money constantly taken by a classmate, the classmate accused him of being "mean." If you find yourself relaxing your boundaries by bending rules or making exceptions to accommodate someone else, it's a good time to consider whether you're dealing with an Emotional Predator.

Before you can modify an Emotional Predator's behavior with rewards for good behaviors and compliance, and sanctions for bad behavior and non-compliance, you must first clearly define "compliance." That means setting boundaries - clear and specific deadlines and benchmarks that you can monitor. Emotional Predators are notorious for delaying, being vague and not responding in a relevant or complete way. If you don't set clear deadlines and benchmarks, you set yourself up to be accused of being unfair or impatient when you act on the Emotional Predator's non-compliance. So state what failure to respond or perform *to a certain fixed standard by a certain date* will mean. Then implement the consequence: positive reward for compliance, negative sanction for non-compliance.

Once you've set a boundary with an Emotional Predator, don't accept or believe excuses unless they're clearly out of her control and truly preventing her from respecting your boundary. Don't rely on her statements of intention or plans for the future. An Emotional Predator will say anything in the moment to get what she wants, and as soon as it serves her to say or do something else, she will. Actions speak louder than words. Look at what other people do, not what they say.

An Emotional Predator is almost certain to test any boundary you set. When she does, it's important that you take steps to enforce your boundary. Setting a boundary that you don't enforce is worse than setting no boundary at all. If you draw a line in the sand with consequences to follow if she crosses it, and then you don't impose those consequences, you teach her that your lines in the sand don't mean anything. So only pick boundaries you're ready, willing and able to enforce, and never threaten anything you can't or won't deliver. Idle threats and bluffs come back to haunt the person who makes them.

Similar to staying unprovoked, setting boundaries with an Emotional Predator can expose him. When your boundary stops him from rolling over you, he becomes frustrated and agitated, and his efforts become more shrill and less slick, which makes his bad behaviors more visible. Sometimes when he thinks he can't get anything from you (because, among other things, you are maintaining firm boundaries), he'll drop his facade altogether and be quite candid about it. Sarcasm, even overt threats, can follow. If you're prepared, you can record them.

Maintaining his facade takes energy, so when an Emotional Predator perceives no return from you for his investment in his facade, he may stop investing in it. A woman I know broke up for the third time with an Emotional Predator boyfriend. As usual, he quickly moved on to a new girlfriend. But this time she set a clear boundary that she wouldn't take him back (by telling him about *her* new boyfriend who she planned to marry). Unlike previous times when she'd broken off with him, this time when he stopped by her house to pick up a few things, he was sullen, grouchy and mean (the opposite of his winsome, fun, happy-go-lucky public persona that he'd used to seduce her over and over). When she asked him, "Is this the real you?", he casually sneered "Yeah. What do you care?". Her boundary exposed him.

Things shift when you set firm boundaries unemotionally. But for some of us, it's difficult to be firm until we've let things get so oppressive that we explode in anger. Reacting in anger makes you a child throwing a tantrum, when you need to be an adult. Being firm isn't being nasty or bitchy, and except in unusual circumstances, it's neither necessary nor helpful to resort to anger to set a boundary. There may be some situations where you decide to strategically *display* anger, but those are rare and risk you being perceived by others as the problem when the Emotional Predator claims to be the victim of your anger "problem."

Getting angry is being provoked, which limits your strategic effectiveness. So never set a boundary or make a request when your anger (or any other emotion) has you in its grip. That doesn't mean you're not entitled to *feel* angry (or anything else). Just don't react or communicate in the grip of intense feelings. *Take every opportunity to respond strategically, rather than react emotionally.*

Like any communication with an Emotional Predator, when you set a limit, be mindful of the words and tone you use. Just state clear deadlines, benchmarks and consequences. Don't editorialize or characterize her behaviors or the limit you are setting. Avoid adjectives or adverbs. Avoid emotional, dramatic or emphatic or absolute words (such as always/never, good/bad, etc...). Avoid sarcasm, put-downs and rhetorical questions (which are often a form of sarcasm) and exclamation point punctuation! Don't explain or justify yourself.

Those communication styles just add your judgments, offering the Emotional Predator a glimpse of your inner state (and making you look bad to anyone else). For example, if you label a particular behavior as "outrageous," you signal to her that the behavior outrages you. If it's outrageous, others will see that more easily from a neutral description of the behavior and circumstance. If you label your boundary as "reasonable," "normal" or "appropriate," you signal your emotional attachment to it. It's enough to simply, concisely and politely state facts, what isn't acceptable to you and what consequences will follow from unacceptable behavior.

While it's a mistake to add your judgments, it's always advisable to use common polite courtesies like "please" and "thank you," particularly when you least feel like using them. Address an Emotional Predator with the style (but not necessarily the content) you'd use to address a boss in a job you can't afford to lose. Treat your communications with (or about) her as business, not personal. A personal diatribe like, "I am sick and tired of your stupid crap. I don't need any more of your outrageous selfishness in my life. Stop calling and don't come here and don't bother me any more ever" isn't going to help. On the other hand, a business-like request like, "Please don't contact me or come to my home or work. Thank you." is a much more effective way to set that boundary. Remember, denigrating the Emotional Predator will leave a paper trail that makes you look bad. And it may provoke more attacks from her.

Sometimes, it's strategically wise to add words to help the Emotional Predator feel like they've won. Don't let your Ego lure you into needing to triumph. For example, "Please don't contact me or come to my home or work. *You deserve more than I can give you. I*

STEP 5 - BE STRATEGIC | 231

wish you the best in all things. Thank you." may satisfy her need to feel superior. Notice how adding that kind of language involves taking a page from the Emotional Predator play book by telling her what she *wants* to hear, rather than what's strictly true for you. She'll tell you what you want to hear when she's seducing you (and when she's recruiting a third party to be her ally, she'll tell them what they want to hear). Use this tactic to your advantage when setting boundaries.

Like any behavior modification, setting boundaries can be done in stages starting with threats and moving through increasingly negative consequences. For example, when you tell an ex-boyfriend not to contact you or come by your house, do it in writing (usually email or texts). If he does it anyway, your next step might be to let him know (again, in writing) that you'll involve the police if he does it again. If he does it again, you can bring your emails or texts to the police station, along with evidence that he did it again (which needs to be more than your word that he contacted you or came by). A quick visit to him from a police officer warning him to keep away from you is often enough to change his behavior. If it isn't, your written requests to him plus the record in the police files of your request for their help is important documentation if you take the next step and ask a court to issue a restraining order.

But before asking police to intervene or seeking a restraining order, assess whether the Emotional Predator will feel he has a face-saving way out. Very sick and violent Emotional Predators can react to police and court intervention as though it's the ultimate, "life and death" assault on their personal autonomy - the ultimate test of their power and independence that backs them into a corner. *If an Emotional Predator has a history of violence or has threatened violence, be very thoughtful before you take any actions that he might perceive as*

*limiting his freedom to do what he wants or as publicly shaming him.
When in doubt, consult an attorney and the police about how to safely
impose a boundary.*

Staying Safe

A word about safety. Bear in mind that one consequence of setting boundaries (and of all strategies for protecting yourself) is that
you are frustrating an Emotional Predator and rejecting her efforts
to use projective identification to transfer her emotional disturbance
to you. As her emotional disturbance remains with her, her agitation grows. At that stage, some Emotional Predators will threaten
violence, or rarely, become violent, both as a way of intimidating you
back into submission and as an uncontrolled outburst of their own
frustration. If you've received physical threats or feel physical violence
is possible, never meet the Emotional Predator in a private location
or without safe witnesses, record every interaction, and always be
emotionally neutral, calm and unprovoked. If you are switching children between your households, meet in a police station lobby or use
an agency set up to facilitate high conflict co-parenting exchanges.

*Always contact local law enforcement if you are threatened or feel
threatened.* Consult an attorney or your local court about getting a restraining order in response to threats or violence. A court may want
clear documentation of an ongoing threat before it'll issue a restraining order, so plan ahead. Long before things reach a crisis, make recordings and have reliable neutral people present to witness abusive
and threatening behaviors. It's better to have recorded many interactions that went okay in order to get on record the one in which the
Emotional Predator bared her fangs, than to have forgotten to make

a recording the one time she shows her true aggressive nature.

Remember that, in any given interaction, the goal of staying safe may conflict with the goal of documenting. If your goal is safety, you may want someone else (or a recording device) there and visible. An Emotional Predator will rarely show her true colors when she thinks anyone can see her, so having a visible witness present can restrain her worst behaviors. If she knows you have a witness present (or you're recording), she's likely to behave better, keeping you safer but thwarting your effort to document bad behavior. So if your goal is safety, have witnesses and recording devices visible to the Emotional Predator. But if your goal is to document bad behavior, a hidden witness or recording device might get you evidence you can use later, but offers less protection in the moment from a violent outburst. And again, use extreme caution backing an Emotional Predator into a corner without leaving her a face saving way out.

THREE CAUTIONS: COURTS, AGENCIES AND INTERNET REVIEWS

Avoid the Courts

It's usually best to avoid the courts whenever possible. Many of us hold a naive belief that courts are places of justice, fairness and truth - a type of modern temple or oracle. For the most part, the courts are run by smart and well-meaning folks. Unfortunately, they aren't likely to understand the true nature of an Emotional Predator problem. And although we want to believe that court decisions are based on facts, rules and justice, they're often based on sound-bite images, shallow first impressions (i.e. "optics"), and an outdated paradigm about human nature.

Courts are a favorite playground of Emotional Predators, where they easily hide their true nature. Court procedures designed to insure fairness offer them almost endless opportunities for the game-playing they love, using technical and arcane court rules to avoid and distract. Court hearings are ideal places to sway a well-intentioned but naive judge (or jury) with plausible emotionally compelling lies based on partial truth and innuendo. And attorney ethical codes require lawyers to present their client's position most favorably. This means omitting information that would give a more complete understanding. Thus *lying by omission is a fundamental and intrinsic lawyer tactic.*

Judges rarely have the time or sophistication to penetrate an Emotional Predator's persuasive facade, and at least in the United States, it's not a judge's role to uncover the facts omitted by an attorney. And time limits in court rarely leave enough time to expose the charming victim facade Emotional Predators present to seduce judges and juries. It takes an Emotional Predator just a moment to throw out shocking accusations and play victim. It can take hours and lots of expensive lawyer time to refute those accusations and offer a more complete and accurate narrative - time that's rarely available in court.

Regrettably, too few lawyers, judges and court system mental health professionals are up to speed about the nature of the modern character-based disturbances that create the vast majority of problems in litigation. Even more disturbing, Emotional Predators are drawn to the power and control of professions in the court system and seek work there as socially sanctioned ways to dominate and bully people.[35] Of course, most people in the court system are good people, but you're more likely to encounter an Emotional Predator there than in other parts of our society. It's a blindside double whammy when the "helpers" themselves suffer the same sort of problem as the difficult clients, and the helpers become part of the problem.

Emotional Predators are particularly at home in the family court system where vague subjective standards like "best interests" and "emotional endangerment" create a no holds barred free-for-all arena to attack their targets where they're most vulnerable: their love for their innocent children. Family court is well known as "liar's court" where sympathetic lies based on partial truth often win the day, regardless of the facts. Persistent high conflict disputes between divorced parents are a feeding ground for parasitic lawyers, therapists, mediators, evaluators and other "experts."

Again, don't get me wrong, there are many hardworking and wonderful family court professionals, but when court system professionals are Emotional Predators themselves, it can become a traumatic nightmare. A client in a situation like that needs to know what Emotional Predators are and steer clear of them even when they appear in the role of an expert helper. *If you can't spot Emotional Predators, you won't be able to determine which authorities and experts don't understand them – or worse are Emotional Predators themselves.*

Although the courts aren't the source of truth, fairness and justice that some of us were brought up to believe, sometimes court can't be avoided or is the only place to get a boundary on an Emotional Predator's behavior. If you do go to court, be well organized and concise, have your facts well documented, have a good lawyer, and present clear evidence that you are the real victim. If you've done a good job documenting the Emotional Predator's previous poor behaviors, it'll help you in court.

Be Prepared for Internet and License Agency Attacks

The internet provides an easy way for Emotional Predators to waste your time and energy. They weaponize tools designed to protect or educate the public (or sell advertising). These days it takes only five minutes and an internet connection for a disturbed person to post negative reviews and complaints. But it can take hours, and sometimes thousands of dollars, to clean up the record.

A client of mine whose ex-husband and his new wife are highly aggressive Emotional Predators found herself attacked by them with fictitious negative internet reviews. It was easy for them to post two nasty paragraphs under fake names pretending to be former clients. She spent time and money contacting former clients for offsetting positive reviews and hiring a lawyer to get an injunction against more of the same from her ex and his new wife.

Professional malpractice and licensing systems are an often overlooked part of the legal system that Emotional Predators use to attack. They're renowned for filing complaints in courts and with licensing agencies. Effortless internet filing now makes licensing grievances a particularly easy tool of harassment. Like negative internet reviews, a disturbed person needs only a few minutes and an internet connection to file a license complaint that can take scores of hours and thousands of dollars in attorney's fees to disprove. Even more than courts, administrative licensing agencies are easily bamboozled by Emotional Predators' distorted emotionally compelling stories. And in the name of protecting "victims" (and justifying their budgets by imposing a large number of sanctions), administrative agencies can ignore facts and common sense and take seriously even the flimsiest and most illogical accusations.

Although there are certainly legitimate reasons to file a court or agency complaint (as we've seen, Emotional Predators are drawn to careers in some licensed professions), those complaints often reflect disturbance in the *complaining* person more than in the person complained about. Complaining about others is a way Emotional Predators avoid taking responsibility for themselves. So while we're routinely told to beware of a professional who's had a complaint filed against her, it's just as important to be cautious when dealing with anyone who has *filed* complaints about professionals. As part of screening, try to find out if a person has filed lawsuits, complaints and grievances.

Neither judges nor administrative agencies are likely to understand the true nature of an Emotional Predator problem. So if you hold a professional license, one way to protect against court and agency abuse is to assume that every client or patient is a hidden Emotional Predator until proven otherwise, and document in client files that you followed all laws and rules governing your profession. Professionals in medicine and law where there's money to be made filing malpractice suits have long understood this. And remember that an Emotional Predator client will tell you what you want to hear (perhaps about your indispensable role as a savior or your exceptional competence) to get you to relax your boundaries and fudge on paperwork or rules. So as we've seen, know your own emotional vulnerabilities well.

chapter eight

Review

"Constant Vigilance!"
Mad Eye Moody, Defense Against the Dark Arts Professor

L et's review some things.

BE REALISTIC ABOUT HUMAN NATURE

As we saw in Part 1, what we call human nature isn't one set of identical traits in all people, stable over different times and cultures. Traits vary with individuals, and it's easy to mistake our unexamined beliefs for intrinsic traits of human nature, rather than the *choices* of culture and upbringing that they are. The first guideline for dealing with Emotional Predators is to *drop your naive belief that because you are generally decent and good, everyone else is basically similar*. In fundamental ways, Emotional Predators are nothing at all like decent people. When you lose sight of this foundational understanding, you become easier prey.[36]

Human nature varies widely between people, and includes a range from marvelous generosity, kindness and caring to chilling greed, barbarity and sadism. Let's hope that our species is improving over time and changing for the better. But for the present, in thinking about Emotional Predators, first and foremost it's essential to expand your notions of what's possible within and from other people. It's not pessimistic to be realistic about the ruthless, unconscionable and selfish manipulation and abuse some people are capable of. That realism is *optimistic* about making life better for yourself and your loved ones.

ACCURATELY ASSESS OTHERS

Once we accept that some people - the Emotional Predators among us - are entirely different from us in core respects, we need to learn how to accurately assess other people. Emotional Predators make their way in life by covering up their true selfish nature, so learn to distinguish between the false *facades* of goodness they present and genuinely good, well-meaning people. To recognize Emotional Predators concealed behind their facades of charm and sincerity, you have to study their tactics, behaviors and attitudes, and how they camouflage themselves.

RECOGNIZE EMOTIONAL PREDATOR TRAITS AND BEHAVIORS

Although they hide it behind charming and deceptive facades, Emotional Predators always ruthlessly use others to get what they want. At their core what they want is power - to feel dominant, winning and in control - and they use a variety of tactics to gratify their drive for power. You should instantly recognize the most common Emotional Predator traits: they *claim to be the victim*, usually of the person they're in fact victimizing; they *fake sincerity and make emotional displays* to influence, intimidate, charm, disarm or seduce others; they *pretend to be innocent and ignorant*; they *trap others in no-win binds* where the other person is damned if they do and damned if they don't; they *provoke others* to act out of character (through passive aggression and projective identification); they *isolate and "gaslight" their targets*, eliciting in the targets unmerited guilt and doubt about their own sanity; they *create havoc, confusion and chaos, and disrupt other people's natural rhythms*; they *ignore rules* when that suits them, but expect others to follow rules when that suits them; they will *say and do anything to get what they want*, reversing themselves later if they think that serves them (they are consummate hypocrites); and they *relentlessly manage their public image*, often by omitting relevant facts (lying by omission).

All Emotional Predators hide, deceive and avoid. They conceal their true nature and objectives, presenting a false image, often very convincingly. They can't be safely relied upon. They misdirect your attention away from what's really important with words and deeds that rarely reflect the full truth. They lie by assertion and omission, for amusement and gain, or simply out of habit. They shift the topic when you try to talk about anything they don't want to address. They avoid giving direct answers to simple questions or requests, and offer excuses and justifications, rather than change. Often there's more accurate information in what an Emotional Predator does *not* say than in what he does say.

The more you can commit these traits and behaviors to memory and recognize them in others, the better protected you'll be. It takes repeated review and experiences to remember new information, so don't worry if you forget. Refer back to resources like this book as often as you need. And rest assured, an Emotional Predator will repeat her behaviors and traits many times.

KNOW YOURSELF

Before you can accurately assess other people, you must know yourself and the blind spots you don't realize you have. They're called *blind* spots because you don't see them - and we all have them. Your blind spots prevent you from seeing Emotional Predators clearly and knowing things about yourself that make you vulnerable. An Emotional Predator will see emotional vulnerabilities in you that you don't notice, and she'll use them against you. Becoming more self-aware reduces the leverage she can apply.

So it's essential to *know yourself better than an Emotional Predator does*. Without noticing it, we create our emotional experience out of the beliefs and stories we choose, and those choices create emotional vulnerabilities. Once you recognize the stories and beliefs you've chosen, you can choose to rid yourself of the self-victimizing core stories and naive beliefs about yourself and others that Emotional Predators exploit.

ADJUST YOUR CORE INTERPERSONAL STORIES

Being flexible about your core stories and values is essential. It's not easy to adjust your core stories about yourself. Those stories generate your identity, your sense of who you are and who you must be to be a good person. But to protect yourself from an Emotional

Predator, you don't need to become someone entirely different. There's no need for an identity crisis. You can make small, but powerful adjustments, becoming more versatile and flexible, developing new capacities and defensive powers you didn't imagine possible.

Start by liberating yourself from your self-victimizing beliefs: the self-defeating stories, self-limiting assumptions and negative self-fulfilling prophesies about yourself and others. A bumper sticker I've always liked says, "Don't believe everything you think." To that I'd add, and don't believe everything you believe. So loosen your grip on stories about yourself and the world that keep you emotionally reactive. Don't be afraid to become a new you.

RESPOND STRATEGICALLY, DON'T REACT EMOTIONALLY

In all matters involving an Emotional Predator, it's essential to *respond strategically, rather than react emotionally*. Your strategic responses restore power to you. Your emotional reactions empower the Emotional Predator. When you reign in your emotional reactions, you can make wiser decisions and regain control. Don't get angry, get smart.

Changing your perspective on events and yourself reduces your emotional reactivity. Whether you experience an event or circumstance as a disaster or good fortune depends on your point of view. Take a long term perspective about success and failure in which the ultimate meaning and impact of events can't be known right now. Today's set back can be tomorrow's inspiration for accomplishment. Who's to say where the events you're going through will lead in the future? Viewed over the long term, there are no mistakes, only opportunities for learning. So, as they say, remain calm and boogie on.

PLAY EMOTIONAL PREDATOR GAMES BETTER THAN THEY DO

Although it may sound shocking, repugnant or distasteful, it's essential to learn to play an Emotional Predator's games better than she does. As they say, *don't bring a knife to a gun fight.* Using Emotional Predator tactics against them doesn't make you an Emotional Predator. They use tactics to get what they want for themselves, with no regard for the negative impact on innocent people. They do this repeatedly as part of an enduring and pervasive pattern of behavior and perception. They're not restrained by empathy or conscience. In contrast, you use those tactics to protect yourself and your loved ones, and you always consider the negative impact on innocent people. You may resort to those tactics under stress or to defend against an Emotional Predator, but you do so temporarily and selectively, not pervasively.[37] Your empathy and conscience always restrain you. Emotional Predators use their tactics for *offense.* You use them for *defense.*

CONTROL INFORMATION

Controlling information is a core Emotional Predator tactic to master. They conceal the truth about themselves and situations, and mine for information about their targets. So learn to play that game better than they do. Like a good poker player, control what the other player knows, particularly about what you really feel and think. Don't be provoked into revealing too much. *Know it, don't show it.* And along with concealing information, improve your information *gathering.* Knowing more about the Emotional Predator and the situation (and about yourself), and having him know less (or less accurately) about you and the situation, is one of the essential guiding principles of protecting yourself. *If you don't control information, you'll undermine all your other efforts.*

PRACTICE DECEPTION

Knowledge is power. So with an Emotional Predator, control as much knowledge as you can. *Practicing deception* is an ancient strategy that's a form of controlling information. Deception involves having accurate knowledge, misdirecting another's attention and keeping your true state concealed. When you can keep an emotional blank screen, you can strategically choose when and what emotions to display and which values and beliefs to show, including emotions you don't actually have and values and beliefs you don't especially value or believe. *Appear strong where you are weak and weak where you are strong, and interested where you are not interested and disinterested where you are interested.* These deceptions let the Emotional Predator waste energy on things that aren't important.

Along with appearing strong where you're weak and weak where you're strong, it's important to *avoid an Emotional Predator where he's strong and engage him where he's weak.* If he has charmed a new teacher or colleague, be wary of trying to persuade that person to see through him. The teacher or colleague may already have been hypnotized, as you were when you first became entangled. Instead of fighting where the Emotional Predator is strong, direct your actions and responses to where he's weak (and to where you're strong). Build relationships with teachers, colleagues and others who haven't been co-opted.

CULTIVATE ALLIES

To that end, it's important to *develop a network of trusted allies* and safe confidants as a reservoir of support for you. An ally could be someone who knows the truth about the Emotional Predator or someone who knows you as a good person and will stand by you. Anticipate when a potential new ally might enter your life and contact them first, framing things in ways that will help the new ally see through the Emotional Predator's facade. The beginning of a school year, the start of a new job, moving to a new neighborhood, the entry of a new colleague or boss are times to consider finding new allies, but you can find them any time. And always screen new people before placing your trust in them, then place your trust slowly and incrementally. Don't unburden your entire story right away. Share a little, test for safety, wait, share some more.

CONSERVE RESOURCES AND AVOID LOSING BATTLES - DO NOT BE PROVOKED

One way Emotional Predators mess with you is getting you to waste your time, money and energy reacting to irrelevant provocations. The specific content of an Emotional Predator's provocation is usually less important than the emotional reaction it triggers. Getting you to react emotionally is a core Emotional Predator goal that serves her primal need to feel powerful, gives her information and weakens you. So save your energy for battles worth fighting.

Emotional Predators love seeing you running around chasing your tail, your attention diverted from what they're really doing. They drain and distract you by spouting irrelevant, irritating and provoking stuff to get you reacting, researching, justifying, explaining or defending yourself about things that are side show distractions. They'll needle you. They'll exhaust you. They'll pressure you through guilt to engage with their nonsense. But engaging on their terms is losing the battle before it's begun. Remember that trying to reason with a crazy person is crazy.

PRACTICE GRATITUDE AND HUMOR

In all things, and particularly in dealing with Emotional Predators, cultivating humor and gratitude is as important as anything else you do. When you're grateful or laughing, you can't feel the negative emotions that Emotional Predators prey on. Humor and gratitude are priceless, free and easily overlooked. They widen your perspective, expand your options, relieve stress and calm you. They immunize you.

In each moment, you can *choose* whether to be grateful or regretful and whether to laugh or cry at the outlandish things an Emotional Predator does; it's a matter of where you focus your attention. That's not to say that you should be grateful for everything or everything is funny. There are certainly plenty of things that aren't so great or funny, but in every moment there also are plenty of things, often very simple things, that you can choose to be grateful for and laugh about.

Every moment offers you many opportunities to laugh and feel grateful. And if you miss the opportunity in one moment, the next moment offers it again. So seek out laughter and gratitude even in the darkest hours. Choose to laugh and appreciate. Control your imagination and attention to help, not hinder, you.

Dealing with an Emotional Predator can feel like a deep tragedy.

But *tragedy is comedy seen from the opposite perspective.* So make every effort to find the humor in what may feel tragic (but don't make fun of an Emotional Predator to his face). *Laughter is one of the greatest, and most easily overlooked, antidotes to toxic adversities in life.* Indulge yourself in it.

chapter nine

Closing Thoughts: Some Paradoxes and Contributing to a More Decent World

"The only thing necessary for the triumph of evil is that good people do nothing." (Attributed to Edmond Burke, but authorship unknown)

Two things can't be stressed enough. First, you have to know yourself (and also the Emotional Predator and the situation) better than the Emotional Predator does - and be willing to change yourself. Second, you need to respond strategically, not react emotionally. Emotional Predators live for your emotional reactions. Provoking you is a fundamental power they seek both for its own thrill and for the information it provides about how to manipulate you.

One paradox of this book is that, while it's all about Emotional Predators, that subject leads us back to *you*. You can't change who an Emotional Predator is. But you can change yourself, and changing yourself can empower you to modify how he *behaves* and insulate you from his remaining toxic behaviors. So know yourself better than an Emotional Predator knows you, and being willing to change. Also paradoxically, the more comfortable you are with not knowing things about yourself and others, the less you'll fill the void of what you don't know with stories that cloud your vision and make you vulnerable.

Another paradox running through this book is that, although Emotional Predators are abominable, to protect yourself and your loved ones, you often need to use their tactics more effectively than they do. This doesn't mean you must *become* an Emotional Predator. It means you can equip yourself with the same weapons they have, and hopefully use them more effectively in your defense.

In order to play Emotional Predators' games better than they do, you need to feel okay standing up for yourself and reject stories about yourself that say you aren't worth protecting. If you've been living a story that devalues you and overvalues others, replace it with one that values you as much as anyone else. Always remember that what other people feel, want and need is important, but it's not more important than what you feel, want and need. So stop treating Emotional Predators the way you'd like to be treated, and start treating every aspect of yourself the way you'd like to be treated.

It's time to change our operative cultural paradigm about interpersonal and social problems, raising standards for human behavior, particularly from government and business leaders, and calling out, ostracizing and penalizing Emotional Predators. In every area of human interaction, it's time to demand decency, empathy, conscience and selfless kindness, and to reject selfishness, deceit, oppression and greed. As more people learn about Emotional Predators and we educate each other, we can update the operative paradigms of our institutions and professions to meet this pressing need of our time.

By recognizing and neutralizing Emotional Predators in your life, you're not only protecting yourself and your loved ones, you're also helping to improve things for everyone. You're contributing to a cultural shift toward new norms of decency, norms that recognize and condemn Emotional Predators for the selfish, conscienceless jerks they are. I hope this book will play a small part in helping you find joy, humor and peace, and immunizing you from the users, abusers and manipulators hidden among us - for your well-being and the well-being of everyone.

Endnotes

1. See May 27, 2010 article by Diane Swanbrow, University of Michigan News.
2. E.g. George Simon, Martha Stout, Robert Hare.
3. In Part 2, I'll explain in detail why using Emotional Predator tactics to protect yourself doesn't make you an Emotional Predator.
4. See Martha Stout *The Sociopath Next Door*; Robert Hare *Without Conscience: The Disturbing World of the Psychopaths Among Us.*
5. See V. S. Ramachandran and others regarding the lesser quantity of mirror neurons in psychopaths.
6. See Jon Ronson, *The Psychopath Test.*
7. Chapter 9 of George Simon's book, *In Sheep's Clothing* describes many of these tactics in short, helpful sections.
8. In *The Dance of Life*, Edward Hall explores the central role of

rhythms in human well-being.

9. From the revised version of an interview of George Soros by Gregor Peter Schmitz, published in the New York Review of Books, Volume LXIII, Number 2, February 11, 2016, at p 36-37. Original interview published in the German magazine WirtschaftsWoche.

10. *In Sheep's Clothing*, revised edition, by George Simon, at pages 112 to 115.

11. Withholding sex as a tactic of manipulation is not the same as avoiding sex for other legitimate reasons that have nothing to do with being an Emotional Predator, such as physical discomfort or past trauma from having been sexually abused. I worked with a woman who was subjected to years of sexual abuse by her Emotional Predator ex-husband. Understandably, she was not always comfortable with sex with her new husband.

12. Jim Edwards, in Business Insider November 24, 2016 article '*The Hare Psychopathy Checklist*': *The test that will tell you if someone is a sociopath.* Available online at http://www.businessinsider.com/hare-psychopath-checklist-test-sociopath-2016-11.

13. The #metoo phenomenon has exposed the widespread extent of sexual abuse in the workplace, which is one pernicious form of Emotional Predator abuse that most people have no trouble identifying when it's brought to their attention.

14. Mike Jay, *The Crime was the Disease*, review in 15 June 2017 London Review of Books.

15. The Rock Man also said, "You gotta open your mind as well as your eyes," and "You gotta get it together - be cool - *dig yourself.*" (Italics added)

16. Carl Jung's theory of the Shadow explores how our emotional reactions point to our blind spots.

17. Thich Nhat Hahn describes Buddhist techniques for transforming anger in *Anger: Wisdom for Cooling the Flames.*

18. EMDR (eye movement desensitization and reprocessing) and BrainSpotting are two widely recommended therapy techniques for resolving trauma, but there are others.

19. The combination of innately impaired empathy and deficient parental mirroring suggests that at least some Emotional Predators are created by a combination of nature and nurture.

20. The Russian language seems to acknowledge two kinds of truth. I've read that "pravda" translates as "empirical or factual truth" (what I call factual truth), and "istina" translates as "transcendental truth" (what I call situational honesty).

21. Guthrie goes on to make the joke, "but think of the *last* guy. He's so low he doesn't have a street to lay in for a truck to run him over." Arlo Guthrie, *The Pause of Mr. Claus.*

22. Jesse Colin Young, *Beautiful.*

23. Doormats who seek Emotional Predators to change, fix or heal can be seen as an expression of the mastery theory of romantic love.

24. Wikipedia entry on Ducking Stools as of November 11, 2017.

25. This was first pointed out to me by Stephen Gallegos, PhD.

26. A detailed instruction for Zen meditating can be found on the website of the Zen Mountain Monastery at https://zmm.mro.org/teachings/meditation-instructions/.

27. Tiffany Watt Smith has explored the ways culture and history have changed how people experience emotions, and how people in different cultures and time periods have had different

emotional reactions to similar situations. In *The Book of Human Emotions* she explores the cultural politics and history of 151 emotions. Her TED talk *The History of Human Emotions* gives a good summary of her ideas about the cultural creation of emotion.

28. This cognitive competence bias is known as the Dunning/Kruger effect.

29. Erich Fromm, *Zen Buddhism and Psychoanalysis*, p 121.

30. A personal favorite of mine is the uncut version of Bradley Cooper on the *Tonight Show with Jimmy Fallon* titled "Bradley Cooper and Jimmy Can't Stop Laughing (uncut version)".

31. This story is from Huai Nan Tzu. Stephen Mitchell tells it in much the same words in the notes to his wonderful translation of Lao Tzu's *Tao Te Ching*.

32. *In Sheep's Clothing*, *The Sociopath Next Door*, *Emotional Vampires*, *Without Conscience*, and this book are my five favorites.

33. Consult local laws about the legality of recording others in your state. When I last checked, in my state you could make secret recordings *of conversations you were a party to*, but it was illegal to secretly record conversations between other people if you were not participating in that conversation. Consult an attorney for the law that applies to you.

34. Technologies evolve quickly. Programs now exist that can create convincing fake videos and photos (i.e. deep fakes), which makes even a photo or video recording subject to doubt about its authenticity. Counter-measures like time and date stamps and independent verification, encryption and block chain storage to assure the veracity of digital recordings are evolving, so you should consult technology and legal experts

about how to insure your recordings are unimpeachable evidence.

35. The part of Chapter 2 about *Empathy* explains why this is so.

36. In his book *Emotional Vampires*, Albert Bernstein puts it this way, "The most dangerous mistake you can make is believing that underneath it all, [these people] are really regular people, just like you. If you interpret what [these people] say and do according to what YOU would feel if you said or did the same thing, you'll be wrong most every time. And you'll end up drained dry."

37. And as mentioned earlier, teenagers also can go through a temporary Emotional Predator-like developmental phase as they experiment with possibilities of social interaction and become for a spell inconsiderate, lazy and manipulative asses.

◆

About the Author

S teven Wolhandler, JD, MA, LPC is a psychotherapist, mediator, arbitrator, custody evaluator, consultant and retired attorney. He has decades of experience dealing with, and learning from, difficult and manipulative people, and helping their victims with penetrating insight, effective solutions, warmth and humor. He lives in Colorado, consults with people nationwide and can be reached through www. emotionalpredators.com and www.creativeresolutions.org.

Printed in Great Britain
by Amazon

51819169R00168